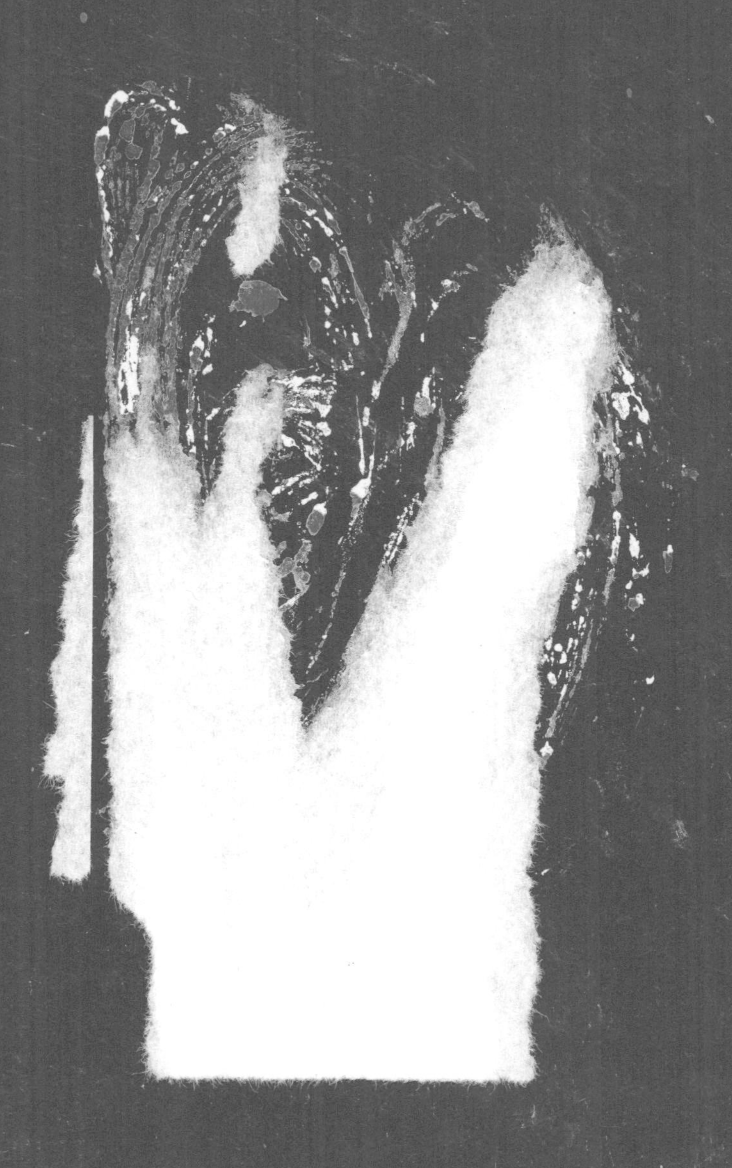

Fat dog slim

Fat dog slim

How to have a healthy, happy pet

Victoria Stilwell

I dedicate this book to my late father, Malcolm Stilwell, who worked so hard to give me the best in life.

First published in 2007 by
Collins, an imprint of
HarperCollinsPublishers
77-85 Fulham Palace Road
Hammersmith
London W6 8JB

The Collins website address is www.collins.co.uk

Collins is a registered trademark of HarperCollins Publishers Ltd

013 012 011 010 09 08 07
7 6 5 4 3 2 1

Photographer: Mark Read
Design: Smith & Gilmour, London
Editors: Barbara Dixon, Joanna Carreras

A catalogue record for this book is available from the British Library

ISBN-13 978-0-00-724920-6
ISBN-10 0-00-724920-9

Collins uses papers that are natural, renewable and recyclable products made from wood grown in sustainable forests. The manufacturing processes conform to the environmental regulations of the country of origin.

Printed and bound in the UK by Butler & Tanner Ltd, Frome

Contents

Introduction

What makes a dog happy? You don't need to be an expert in animal behaviour to figure it out, he'll tell you himself. Nine times out of ten what triggers the eager expression, wagging tail and excited barks that dogs use to signal pleasure are a few very simple things. Food. Exercise. And company (human and canine).

What makes a dog healthy? Well, it's the same as the above, but with certain qualifications. He needs the right food, in the *right* quantities. He needs a decent amount of exercise, tailored to his age and breed. He needs a variety of stimulating experiences to keep him mentally alert and healthy in the widest sense of the word.

In the wild, dogs provide for themselves. The whole business of survival – working in a pack to track down prey – delivers what they need in one complete package: nourishment, physical conditioning and social interaction. Our domestic pets can't go to the supermarket, let themselves out of the house, or arrange a get-together. They have to rely on us.

When you bring a dog into your home you are making a commitment. As his owner, you are responsible for his wellbeing, you are your dog's teacher and ultimate leader. One of those responsibilities is to get informed, so that you know you are doing the best you can to give him a healthy, active life. We've all read those harrowing cases of animal cruelty that make headlines in the press and keep charities working overtime. But many owners short-change their pets without intending to harm them in any way, and they often do so precisely because they *love* them.

Let's take a simple example. It's been estimated that almost 40 per cent of domestic dogs are overweight and a shocking 25 per cent are obese. Why should these statistics concern us? Fat dogs, like fat people, are at serious medical risk. They are less likely to survive operations and more susceptible to conditions that result from the stress the extra weight places on their joints, heart, lungs, liver and kidneys. For all these reasons, an overweight dog is less likely to live out his full lifespan than a dog who is fit and trim. Just like people, in fact.

No one sets out to make their dog sick or shorten his life. Sometimes people simply haven't got the information they need to feed their dog a good diet or look after him properly. But all too often problems arise because owners treat their dogs as if they were human beings. They 'pamper' them with the same unhealthy snacks they eat themselves without any idea what that type of diet is doing to their pet's long-term health. They gaze into those pleading doggy eyes and hand over a biscuit (and I don't mean a dog biscuit). Of course, dogs have been fed table scraps for centuries. But table scraps in this day and age may come in the form of sugary, fatty, processed food that isn't doing humans any more favours than it is dogs. Factor in our increasingly sedentary lifestyle and it isn't just people who become couch potatoes. It's also the dogs snuggled up there on the sofa alongside them.

It's pretty easy to see that overweight, under-exercised dogs are not in the peak of condition. A truly healthy dog, however, is not merely the right weight for his size and breed, he's also receiving the right nutrients in a properly digestible form. Aggression and hyperactivity are just two of the 'behavioural' problems that can have dietary causes. Dogs fed on poor-quality, highly processed, 'convenience' dog food can wind up malnourished and suffering many preventable illnesses and disorders.

I've worked with dogs all my adult life. I've been a dog-walker and dog-sitter; I've worked with rescue shelters on both sides of the Atlantic and I've fostered many dogs myself, nurturing and rehabilitating dogs that have been abandoned or abused. In my present capacity as a dog-trainer and behavioural advisor, I've seen all sorts of problems, but I've rarely met a 'bad' dog. What I do encounter regularly are owners who are having difficulties with their pets because they don't understand what makes them tick. It's a theme that crops up over and over again in the families I advise on the television programme *It's Me or the Dog*.

Understanding dog behaviour is the key to successful, positive training and it's the entire basis of my approach. In the same way, to raise and nurture a happy, active pet, you need to know exactly what his physical requirements are and be prepared to meet these every day. It will mean viewing the claims of some pet-food manufacturers with the same healthy scepticism you would view any mass-marketed product. It will mean training your dog properly so he will come when he's called, socialise with other dogs and humans safely and enjoy every dog's birthright – a glorious run off the lead. It will mean taking the time to play with your dog, to stimulate his senses and provide him with a variety of experiences to keep boredom at bay.

This book is intended to be a comprehensive guide to the three essential aspects of canine health and happiness – diet, exercise and stimulation. You can use it as a fitness programme to get your dog back on track. You can find out how to adjust feeding and exercise to suit the needs of an older pet, or you can treat it as a manual for rearing a new puppy to adulthood. Whichever is the case, when you pull it all together you will set your dog up for the best life you could possibly give him. When you think what dogs give us, and how rewarding it is to share our lives with them, it's the least we can do!

Teaching your dog

Basic obedience training gives your dog the important skills that he will need to live successfully in our human world. Some people mistake training for domination or browbeating a dog into submission. Others think that teaching a dog to give his paw, for example, is demeaning. Neither is the case. Positive training strengthens the bond between you and your dog and gives your dog boundaries so that he knows how he is expected to behave. A well-trained dog is confident, alert, happy and relaxed.

Throughout the book, I have included instructions on how to teach your dog key commands. These have obvious relevance to canine health and fitness. If you teach your dog to SIT and wait for his food, for example, you teach him valuable impulse control and reinforce the message that you are the one in charge of this important resource. When a dog has mastered the COME command, he'll be able to look forward to many happy runs off the lead. All training is good mental stimulation for dogs – and they need that as much as we do.

All my training techniques are positive. I never use hard punishment and nor should you. I use rewards – food treats, toys, more fun – to reward good behaviour (whether I asked for it or not). I use short, sharp vocal corrections or a distracting noise to alert the dog he hasn't behaved the way he was supposed to. The word 'no' has no role in positive training. During training I say 'uh oh!' when a dog doesn't do what he's been asked and, if I am training with a treat, I remove the treat from view. I also say 'ah ah!' in a guttural voice when a dog misbehaves.

You need to use both vocal cues and physical signals in dog training. Dogs watch us more than they listen to us. A clear hand signal can be picked up by a dog a long way away, while our voices often don't carry that far. When you train a dog to perform a specific task, you link a word and gesture to a particular behaviour and reinforce the association with praise and/or a treat.

The absolute key to successful training is timing. Dogs will only associate a certain behaviour with a reward or correction if the time between the two is very short. One second, no more. As soon as your dog gives his paw or puts his rear on the floor, or whatever you've asked him to do, reward him immediately. If you don't catch the precise action, your dog will think he's getting rewarded or corrected for something else entirely.

Here are some tips for training:

- Keep sessions short. Five to ten minutes three times a day is better than lengthy periods of training.
- Start training early – as soon as you bring your puppy home. And carry on training all through your dog's life.
- Once you have started training, don't give a food or toy reward to the dog every single time he gets something right. Always give him praise, but reward intermittently. This adds value to the reward and makes your dog learn faster. It also allows the possibility for improvement.
- Vary the rewards you give. In addition to food treats, you can give toys, as well as petting, play and exercise.
- Think about your dog's basic physique before teaching him certain commands. If he has hip problems, for example, don't make him sit for long periods.
- Make training fun and playful. When a dog senses you are enjoying yourself, he will, too. Adopt an energetic and enthusiastic manner to keep your dog interested.
- Never manipulate the dog physically into doing what you want him to do. He should do the mental work to figure it out and get the reward.
- Pick your training times carefully. Tired dogs don't learn easily. Dogs that have just had dinner won't be motivated as strongly by food treats as those that are a little hungrier.
- Be consistent. Everyone who works with the dog should use the same commands and signals.
- Vary the picture. If you only teach your dog in the kitchen, he won't necessarily obey you elsewhere. Start training him somewhere quiet where there are no distractions, then move to other places around the home. Eventually, move outdoors and train your dog in surroundings where there is more going on. In the same way, vary your body positions. Use the same command and the same gesture or signal but adopt different postures – sitting or crouching, for example.
- As training progresses, increase your distance from your dog. Only give a command or a signal once.
- Be patient. You don't need special equipment to train a dog successfully, but you do need lots of patience.

chapter one

chow time

When dogs first came to live with humans, they awarded themselves and their descendants a massive advantage. As the world's most successful species, man was the ultimate protector; ever since the human–dog partnership began, our four-legged friends have enjoyed a security that would never have been their lot in the wild.

It is thought that this great double act initially joined forces around 15,000 years ago, when the first human settlements were made. It was probably food that made the introduction. Nomadic life meant that our ancestors could move away from their rubbish. But as soon as people started settling in one spot the bones and food waste they discarded must have represented easy pickings for scavenging wolves, with the result that the bolder ones soon found themselves with human companions. And vice versa.

After dogs left the wilderness behind they chiefly survived on leavings from the human table, scraps and bones and whatever they could scavenge. Then, about a century or so ago, something happened to change that state of affairs.

Your dog is what he eats

Within a relatively short space of time, manufactured dog food, generally produced from waste products of the human food industry, became the standard diet of the domestic dog. Today, most dog owners rely on some form of pet food – dried, canned, semi-moist or 'gourmet' – to feed their dogs, often to the exclusion of anything else.

But over the same short period, something else happened. Dogs began to get ill with diseases that had never been that prevalent in the species before – digestive diseases such as diabetes and pancreatitis, as well as degenerative conditions of the heart, lungs and liver. In fact, the same kind of diseases that have gone hand in hand with the contemporary Western lifestyle and our excessive consumption of highly processed food.

As a dog-lover I care enough for their wellbeing to think long and hard about the nutritional value of what I give them to eat. As a dog-trainer and behavioural advisor, one of the first questions I ask my clients concerns the diet they routinely feed their dogs. What I find is that the answers often have a bearing on the type of problems they're experiencing with their pets. My research – which started when I first read the list of ingredients on the back of a can of dog food and wondered what on earth they meant – tells me that an awful lot of what is marketed as healthy pet food is anything but. The packaging is great, the endorsements are persuasive, and a cute advertising campaign shows happy dogs with shiny coats and bright eyes wolfing the food down with gusto. The product is not only competitively priced, you can pick it up almost anywhere. Scratch the surface, however, and decode some of those terms listed on the product label, and you might not be so quick to put the food in your supermarket trolley or your dog's bowl.

To be absolutely blunt, what chiefly sells mass-market pet food is convenience. For people, that is, not dogs. You pick your brand, order or buy it in bulk, dish it up every day and that takes care of feeding the dog. End of story.

Except it isn't the end of the story. Your dog isn't satisfied with his dinner, he wants yours – but that's no surprise, is it? Most dogs love food, we all know that. But then comes a steady stream of ailments . . . allergies, skin conditions, dental problems, diarrhoea, and possibly a more serious condition you didn't even know dogs could get. And the vet bills mount up.

Your dog is what he eats. Feed him the right diet and you've given him a huge head start to lifelong health and fitness.

So what is the correct diet? Some people believe the right way to feed dogs is to give them an exclusively raw diet based on uncooked meaty bones. Others feed their dogs human food they have cooked themselves. Then there are the many different commercial brands that the overwhelming majority rely on, ranging from natural, organic products to highly processed foods with highly dubious ingredients. Wet or dry? Premium, gourmet, or supermarket own-brand? How do you know what is best?

I recommend feeding a dog very high-quality dog food, both wet and dry, which contains ingredients you can trust. I would supplement this with a little cooked chicken and cooked vegetables, chiefly to provide variety of taste and texture. The homemade food option might be worth exploring if you have the time to source the ingredients, weigh them out in the correct quantities and prepare them – but most people don't. What is important is that your dog gets the best possible deal at chow time you can give him. Later in the chapter I'll be showing you how to tell a good dog food from a downright mediocre one so you can make your own selection, or go the DIY route if that's what you choose.

A balanced diet

Unlike the domestic cat, whose ancestors were pure carnivores, a dog is by nature more omnivorous. A dog's sharp canine teeth might appear to mark him out primarily as a meat-eater, but when wild dogs devour their animal prey, they consume the whole carcass, which includes bones, offal and the contents of the stomach and intestinal tract. In fact, wild dogs go for the stomach and its contents first, which chiefly consist of partially digested vegetable matter. Yes, dogs eat vegetables.

There has been some debate about whether the dog's nutritional needs have evolved during the course of their long association with humans – whether they have become more omnivorous over time. Dogs are almost entirely dependent on what their human companions give them, more so than cats, which will hunt and eat wild prey given the opportunity. Selective breeding has also resulted in dramatic changes to the canine species. Neither the Great Dane nor the Pekingese bears much outward resemblance to their wolf ancestors, after all. But it seems likely that wild dogs have always had a more varied diet than their popular reputation as slathering meat-eaters would seem to suggest. Dogs love meat, but a dog fed exclusively on meat will end up deficient in several important nutrients, including calcium and a number of key vitamins. At the same time, a meat-only diet contains excessive amounts of protein. Too much protein in the diet has been linked with higher levels of aggression and hyperactivity.

A great deal of research has been carried out in the field of dog nutrition in recent years and, although there remain some lively areas of disagreement, most experts agree that dogs need a balanced diet that includes all the main food groups, just like humans. In other words, they require protein, carbohydrate, fats, vitamins and minerals. Most importantly, however, they need those nutrients in an easily digestible form, otherwise their bodies can't use them.

But that's only part of the story. To feed your dog correctly you also have to take into account his specific needs – his age, level of activity and, in some cases, breed, variables that I'll cover in a later chapter.

Protein

The general consensus is that about 20 per cent of an adult dog's daily calorie intake should be protein. Lactating females, puppies, very active working dogs and older dogs have different protein needs (see Chapter Two, page 58).

Proteins are composed of amino acids, which are essential for a dog's health and growth. Ten of these – arginine, histidine, isoleucine, leucine, lysine, methionine, phenylalanine, threonine, tryptophan and valine – can only be obtained through what a dog eats. Amino acids perform a vast range of functions in the body, from bone formation to the production of red blood cells, and also have a direct bearing on mood, performance and the maintenance of a healthy immune system.

Many of the amino acids that a dog needs can only be found in animal protein, such as meat, fish and dairy products. Cereal proteins, derived from corn, wheat and soy, are less readily digestible by the dog and can result in allergic reactions and actual protein deficiency because the nutrients aren't being absorbed. Signs of protein deficiency include so-called 'behavioural' problems such as spinning or tail chewing, timidity and aggression (confusingly, also a sign that a dog is eating too much meat), as well as lethargy and lack of appetite. Excessive shedding, brittle toenails, skin and ear infections, and stomach upsets also indicate too little animal protein in the diet. The dog may eventually develop more serious conditions, including hormonal, reproductive and organ malfunction. Too much protein in the diet, as mentioned before, can cause hyperactivity and aggression. It will also put a strain on the dog's kidneys because the body will be forced to use the protein as a main energy source.

Carbohydrate

Carbohydrates – starchy foods such as pasta, potatoes, rice and root vegetables – are energy-giving foods. In the wild, dogs do eat carbohydrates which can be an element of the stomach contents of their prey, for example. However, this food group makes up less than a third of their diet; in commercial pet food, that proportion can be almost double. The reason is that carbohydrate is a cheaper energy source than protein and helps to bulk out the food.

As far as dogs are concerned, there are good carbohydrates and bad. Best, because it is easiest to digest, is rice. Oats and peas are other good sources. Corn and wheat are not easily digested by dogs and can cause problems such as allergies and bloating. Sugar, added to some pet foods to improve the taste, can make dogs pile on the pounds just like humans.

A dog that is fed a diet that is very high in carbohydrates will show signs of protein deficiency and may become overweight. Carbohydrates take more time to digest and create more waste, which puts a dog's body under strain.

Fibre

Carbohydrates that are high in fibre are particularly valuable and can help prevent diseases such as diverticulitis. Because fibre takes longer to digest and doesn't rush through the dog's system, it helps manage conditions that affect blood sugar levels, such as diabetes. Between 2.5 per cent and 4.5 per cent of a dog's calorie intake should consist of food high in fibre.

Fat

Fat performs a number of important functions in the dog's body. It allows other nutrients to be absorbed, particularly the fat-soluble vitamins A, D, E and K; it keeps cells strong and resistant to infection and it promotes a healthy skin and coat. Fat also plays an important role in the nervous system and in the regulation of body temperature. And, of course, fat is also a source of energy.

Fat contains three ingredients that a dog needs, namely, linoleic acid, linolenic acid and arachidonic acid. These fatty acids, which can only be obtained through what a dog eats, can be obtained either from saturated (or animal) fats or from polyunsaturated (or vegetable) fats. Dogs need a mixture of both. Deficiencies of saturated fats show up in lethargy, poor growth, heart problems and dry skin. Too much saturated fat leads to obesity and some types of cancer. Deficiencies of polyunsaturated fats cause skin lesions and other skin problems, a coarse, dry coat and poor blood clotting.

How much fat a dog needs in his diet varies according to his age and level of activity. The range is between 5 and 20 per cent fat, with puppies needing more and older dogs needing less. An adult pet would benefit from a diet that contains only a relatively small proportion of fat.

Minerals and vitamins

Just like humans, dogs that don't eat food that is rich in the right vitamins and minerals suffer deficiencies that may show up in poor condition or behavioural problems. Supplementation can sometimes be the answer, but you should only give your dog extra vitamins and minerals on a vet's advice. In some cases, an excess of a mineral in the diet can be just as bad as a deficiency; problems caused by excesses of vitamins are rare to non-existent.

The minerals and vitamins essential for a dog's health and the functioning of his metabolism are listed on pages 26–29. Bear in mind that requirements can vary according to the age of the dog and his level of activity, or in the case of a female dog, whether she is pregnant or lactating.

Water

Dogs can survive for quite some time without food but they quickly get into serious difficulty without water. A dog that loses 15 per cent of the total water content in his body will die – and a dog's body is 60–70 per cent water. Water is necessary to regulate body temperature and to keep acid levels constant in the blood. It's also a key part of the digestive process, allowing nutrients to be absorbed and flushing out toxins from the system.

Fresh drinking water must be available to a dog at all times. Dogs naturally drink more in hot weather or after prolonged exercise, so you will have to keep an eye out and top up the bowl more often. Carry a water supply with you if you are travelling with your pet.

How much a dog drinks will also be affected by the kind of food you feed him. Feeding a dog dry food, which may contain as little as 10 per cent moisture, will increase his thirst. Canned food, on the other hand, may be 80 per cent moisture, which will mean a dog will drink much less.

Dogs dehydrate very quickly when they are deprived of water. Illnesses that produce vomiting or diarrhoea often result in rapid dehydration.

Signs of dehydration include:

- The skin becomes less elastic. Pinch your dog's skin between your thumb and finger and pull it up. When you release it, it should fall back into place more or less straight away. In dehydrated dogs, the skin takes longer to return to normal.
- Dry, sunken eyes.
- Dry mouth, gums and nose.
- Pale gums. Press your finger against your dog's gums. The pressure will produce a white patch. In a normal dog that white patch will return to a healthy pink as soon as you take your finger away. In a dehydrated dog, it may take up to three seconds to return to normal.

MINERALS

Twelve minerals are essential for dogs. Calcium, phosphorus, magnesium, potassium, sodium and chloride are required in greater amounts than copper, iodine, iron, manganese, selenium and zinc.

CALCIUM

Calcium is a very important mineral for a dog and is required in larger amounts than other minerals. Feeding a dog a diet rich in meat can lead to a calcium deficiency and can also upset the balance between phosphorus and calcium, a ratio that is crucial in dogs. The correct ratio is 1.2 parts of calcium to 1 part of phosphorus.
Found in: Bones and bone meal, dairy products, peas, beans and lentils
Function: Formation of bones and teeth; also important for blood, nerves and muscle
Deficiency: Skeletal problems such as rickets
Excess: Bone problems in growing dogs, especially those of large breeds

PHOSPHORUS

Without the correct amount of phosphorus in the diet, calcium cannot be used by the body, even if it is present in the right quantity.
Found in: Meat, including organ meat, eggs, milk
Function: Skeletal growth; maintaining healthy bones
Deficiency: Rare
Excess: Accelerates kidney failure

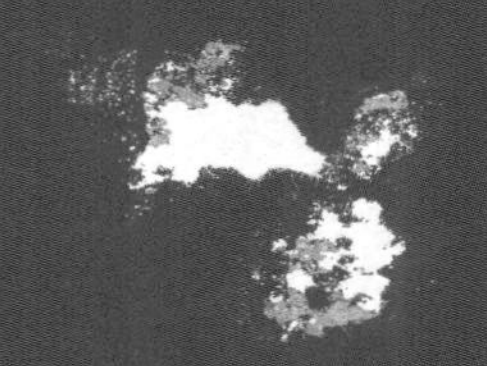

MAGNESIUM

Absorption of this mineral is dependent on calcium and phosphorus being present in the correct ratio.
Found in: Whole grains, soya, raw wheat germ, milk, fish
Function: Promotes the absorption and use of other minerals and vitamins; enzyme and hormone function; bone growth
Deficiency: Rare
Excess: Rare

POTASSIUM

Because potassium is found in many different foods, including pet food, deficiencies are almost always due to diseases that cause potassium to be lost from the body. Prolonged bouts of diarrhoea and/or vomiting can bring potassium levels dangerously low.
Found in: Many foods; high in whole grains, bran and yeast
Function: Maintaining fluid balance; enzyme function; muscles and nerves
Deficiency: Heart failure; nervous disorders; weakness and loss of appetite
Excess: Rare if the kidneys are functioning normally

SODIUM AND CHLORIDE

Sodium chloride (table salt) is found in most foods and is added to pet food as a flavour-enhancer. Most pet foods contain much higher levels than the recommended minimum. As is the case with potassium, dietary deficiencies are rare. Those caused by prolonged vomiting and diarrhoea can be very serious. If a dog does not have access to clean drinking water, levels can rise dangerously high, leading to seizures and death in a short space of time.
Found in: Nearly all foods, including pet food
Function: Maintaining fluid balance; maintaining acid/alkali balance
Deficiency: Rare
Excess: Rare

COPPER
Some breeds, including West Highland white terriers, Doberman pinschers and Bedlington terriers, have a hereditary disorder that causes copper to build up in the liver (where it is generally stored). This can result in hepatitis.
Found in: Fish, liver, peas, beans and lentils, whole grains
Function: Formation of connective tissue; development of red blood cells and hair pigment; iron absorption
Deficiency: Rare
Excess: Rare, except in certain breeds (see above)

IODINE
Iodine helps to control the metabolic rate and promote growth.
Found in: Fish, iodised salt, eggs
Function: Promotes the function of the thyroid gland
Deficiency: Weight gain; weakness; hair loss; poor growth
Excess: Scurf; excessive saliva; excessive discharge from tear ducts and nose

IRON
Iron is a key mineral for producing healthy red blood cells.
Found in: Meat, liver, whole grains, peas, beans, lentils, fish
Function: Producing haemoglobin; enzyme function
Deficiency: Anaemia
Excess: Rare

MANGANESE
Manganese allows the body to make proper use of the protein and carbohydrate in the diet.
Found in: Green vegetables, whole grains, seeds, eggs
Function: Enzyme function; important in reproduction
Deficiency: Rare
Excess: Unknown

SELENIUM
Very little selenium is required by dogs.
Found in: Meat, cereals
Function: Helps to protect cells; helps bolster the immune system
Deficiency: Rare
Excess: Rare

ZINC
Zinc is hard to absorb. Northern breeds, such as huskies, can find it harder to absorb the zinc they need.
Found in: Meat, bone
Function: Enzyme function; skin health; promotes healing
Deficiency: Skin lesions; dull, dry coat; hair loss; weight loss
Excess: Rare

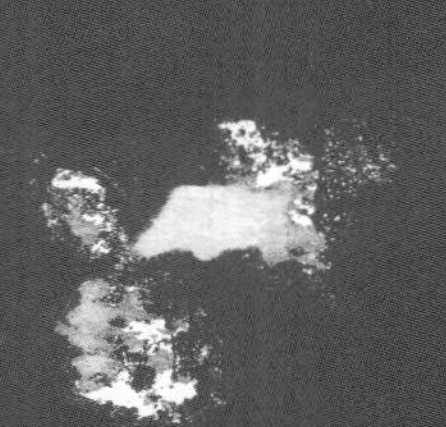

VITAMINS

Vitamins work with minerals in countless ways to promote and maintain bodily functions. There are two main kinds: those that are water-soluble (Vitamin C and the B complex vitamins) and those that are fat-soluble and can be stored in the body (Vitamin A, Vitamin D, Vitamin E and Vitamin K). Vitamin deficiencies are much more serious and common than excesses, which are very rare.

VITAMIN A

Vitamin A is chiefly stored in the fat cells in the liver. The first milk or colostrum is rich in Vitamin A and it is a very important vitamin for growing puppies.
Found in: Yellow vegetables (as carotene), liver, cod liver oil, dairy products
Function: Important for vision, growth, healthy skin and coat
Deficiency: Stunted growth; reproductive problems; night blindness; poor skin and fur
Excess: Rare

VITAMIN B1 (THIAMIN)

Like all the B complex vitamins, thiamin is not stored in the body, which means the diet needs to provide sufficient amounts on a daily basis. Raw fish contains an enzyme that destroys thiamin.
Found in: Meat, fish, vegetables, milk and fruit
Function: Converts glucose to energy
Deficiency: Weakness; loss of appetite; poor reflexes; neural disorder; in extreme cases death
Excess: None

VITAMIN B2 (RIBOFLAVIN)

Dogs on vegetarian diets may need supplements of this key vitamin.
Found in: Organ meat, dairy products
Function: Promotes normal growth and healthy coat
Deficiency: Collapsing and weakness of rear limbs; poor growth; vision problems; heart failure
Excess: None

VITAMIN B3 (NIACIN)

Another B complex vitamin, niacin is very important for health. Because it is chiefly found in meat, dogs on vegetarian diets may need supplementation.
Found in: Meat
Function: Enzyme function
Deficiency: Weight loss; inflammation of gums, cheeks and lips; diarrhoea; in extreme cases death
Excess: None

VITAMIN B5 (PANTOTHENIC ACID)

This B complex vitamin can be destroyed by processing.
Found in: Raw meat and vegetables
Function: Helps convert protein, carbohydrate and fat into energy
Deficiency: Digestive disorders; diarrhoea; hair loss
Excess: None

VITAMIN B6 (PYRIDOXINE)

Often destroyed by processing, B6 is an extremely important vitamin.
Found in: A wide range of foods
Function: Helps the body make use of the amino acids found in protein
Deficiency: A wide range of disorders including tooth decay, sores, anaemia and poor growth
Excess: None

VITAMIN B7 (BIOTIN)

Raw egg whites contain an enzyme that destroys biotin; raw yolks, however, are very rich in it. If you want to feed your dog raw egg, feed the yolk only.

Found in: Beef liver, brewer's yeast, raw egg yolk
Function: Aids growth, digestion; maintains skin and coat
Deficiency: Poor coat; sores; diarrhoea
Excess: None

VITAMIN B12 AND FOLIC ACID

These vitamins work together to produce red blood cells.

Found in: Organ meat
Function: Production of red blood cells
Deficiency: Anaemia
Excess: None

VITAMIN C (ASCORBIC ACID)

Healthy dogs are able to produce this vitamin themselves from glucose, but it is added to pet food as a natural preservative. It may also be given as a supplement to puppies or lactating females.

Found in: Citrus fruits and vegetables
Function: Bone formation and growth
Deficiency: Weak bones and swollen joints (scurvy)
Excess: None

VITAMIN D

Dogs gain Vitamin D both from their diet and from sunshine.

Found in: Exposure to ultraviolet radiation, liver, fish oils, dairy products
Function: Regulates levels of calcium and phosphorus
Deficiency: Poor bone formation (rickets)
Excess: Rare

VITAMIN E

As an antioxidant, Vitamin E can be added to pet food as a preservative.

Found in: Meat, including liver; vegetable oils, nuts, leafy vegetables
Function: Important for the formation of cells and cell function
Deficiency: Damaged organ tissue; ulcerated bowels
Excess: None

VITAMIN K

Like Vitamin C, Vitamin K is produced in the dog's body and supplementation is not necessary.

Found in: Green plants and vegetables, kelp, egg yolk
Function: Regulates blood clotting
Excess: None

Dogs' dinners

Knowing what constitutes good dog nutrition is all very well, but how do you translate those percentages into a healthy meal for your pet? How do you make sure he gets what he needs?

If you watch what you eat and what you feed your family, read the backs of packets and tins with a wary eye for additives and chemicals and are generally clued up on the subject of healthy eating, you'll have no difficulty extending the same approach to your pet. If not – maybe it's time you shook up your own eating habits and made the effort to be kind to yourself as well as your dog!

Variety is the spice of life

Many owners think that it makes no difference if they feed their dogs the same food day after day. After all, the dog doesn't complain and he never leaves anything in his bowl. But what happens if that same dog is offered a choice between a strip of cooked beef and a handful of his usual kibble? I know which one he'll go for first.

We have four times more taste buds than dogs, but that does not mean dogs do not gain sensory pleasure from their food. In the dog, the taste buds are located on the tongue, on the soft palate and at the back of the throat. Different areas are sensitive to different tastes: the sweet taste buds are on the side of the tongue, the sour and salty ones further back on the sides. The front two-thirds of the tongue are for meaty tastes, while bitter tastes are sensed at the back of the tongue. The taste buds at the tip of the tongue are sensitive to water.

In food tests, dogs have been shown to prefer meat to vegetables and beef and pork to lamb and chicken. They also favour wet over dry food, possibly because they find wet food easier to taste. Warm food, which tastes and smells stronger, is similarly preferred to cold food. Dogs have also been shown to favour new tastes over ones that are familiar, which is good for survival as it ensures that given the chance they will eat many different types of food and benefit from the broadest range of nutrients.

And while dogs have fewer taste buds than humans, their sense of smell is awesome. The dog has forty times more sensory receptors in his nose and nasal cavities than we do. He may not taste the same subtleties of flavour when he's eating the food, but its smell will speak volumes to him. 'Mouthing' is also an important exploratory tool for a dog. He will investigate something by putting it in his mouth and feeling its shape and texture. For all these reasons, if you give a dog the same food day in day out you are depriving him of sensory pleasure on a whole range of fronts.

Many people feed their dogs exclusively on dry food. It's generally cheaper, more convenient and produces less smelly stools. But feeding a dog a completely dry diet can lead to problems such as excessive thirst (and increased urination), dry skin, bloating and flatulence, while a diet that is solely composed of wet food doesn't offer the crunchy texture that dogs enjoy.

I recommend feeding dogs both wet and dry food to make sure they experience different textures. I would also offer cooked chicken and cooked vegetables such as carrots, cabbage and broccoli from time to time. That's not because I don't trust the prepared food to deliver what they need, it's to give them the pleasure of variety.

However, while you can offer different flavours, I wouldn't recommend that you chop and change brands all the time in the interests of variety. Once you have found a good product that suits your dog, give thanks and stick with it. Dramatically altering diet on a regular basis can throw a dog's digestion out of kilter.

Commercial dog food

Good, mediocre or downright awful, commercially available dog food varies widely in quality. Pet food is big business, worth over $11 billion a year in the United States and £1.5 billion in Britain alone. Leading manufacturers make use of the same persuaders to sell their brands as companies selling food for human consumption. Nine times out of ten when you buy a well-known brand, you're paying as much for the advertising, promotion and packaging as you are for the basic ingredients. Most of the leading pet-food companies are subsidiaries of major multinationals, turning by-products from the human food industry into profit.

There is such a thing as high-quality dog food and the market is expanding as demand increases. You may have to search harder for it (although the internet takes the legwork out of research these days), and you will almost certainly have to pay more for it. The increased cost, however, is offset by the fact that these foods are so nutritious that dogs require smaller quantities to be satisfied. Be wary of those pet foods advertised as 'gourmet' or 'premium'. These do not always live up to their glitzy packaging.

Dogs (and their human owners) have been short-changed too long by inadequate food dressed up as the perfect, complete diet. But consumer choice has a real power to change things for the better. The more we scrutinise what goes into popular brands and seek out healthier alternatives, the quicker the industry will sit up and take notice.

Be wary of those pet foods advertised as 'gourmet' or 'premium'. These do not always live up to their glitzy packaging.

What makes a good dog food?

The basis of any good dog food is high-quality ingredients. The meat should come from a reliable source and from animals that are fit for human consumption. The method of processing is another key factor. Slow cooking at low temperatures under vacuum conditions preserves as much of the nutritional value of the ingredients as possible. Preservatives should be natural ones such as Vitamin C, Vitamin E and rosemary. If a food has been naturally preserved, it should be eaten between four and six months from the time of manufacture.

The brands I feed my dogs use natural organic ingredients. They are hypo-allergenic, which means they do not contain ingredients that have been shown to cause adverse or allergic reactions in dogs. They contain a good percentage of high-quality animal protein and the carbohydrate content is chiefly rice, which is easy to digest. They also contain no artificial flavourings, colourings, or preservatives.

How to read a label

In order to tell the difference between a high-quality dog food and an inadequate one, you will have to learn to translate some of those confusing terms on the back of the packet or tin. Manufacturers are legally bound to list what their products contain, but that does not mean that the pet-food industry is as well regulated as it should be. On some dog foods you will find vague terms such as 'by-product' or 'derivative'. One of the reasons such terms are used is because manufacturers don't want you to know exactly what is in the food. Another reason is that they can switch to a cheaper source of protein, for example, when they want to. That's why some dogs that have done OK on a particular brand for a while can suddenly develop an intolerance. It's not the dog that's changed, it's what's in the tin or packet.

Besides which, we have no way of knowing if pet-grade meat or meat 'by-products' (there's a euphemism for you!) come from animals that were diseased or heavily dosed with hormones, steroids, antibiotics and other chemicals. I don't want those chemicals in my system and I certainly don't want them in that of my dog.

It all begins with the product description. Canned foods labelled 'beef dinner' or 'chicken stew' may contain very little meat. Products labelled 'beef flavour' may contain no beef at all. Generally the first ingredient listed on the label is what the product is chiefly made of. But even if some form of meat heads the list – say, chicken, lamb or beef – a large percentage of that meat may actually be water, especially if the food is relatively cheap. A common way of processing meat for low-grade pet food is to cook it at very high temperatures and under extreme pressure, which can destroy vital amino acids and digestive enzymes in the protein.

Here are some other common terms:

- Meat (chicken, lamb or beef). Meat that has been ground into small particles.
- By-products. Meat by-products are those parts of an animal carcass that are deemed unfit for human consumption. These include heads, feet, tails, hair, ligaments, bones, intestines, lungs and so on. Chicken by-products include necks, feet, intestines, organs, undeveloped eggs, heads and beaks – even the odd feather that has found its way into the processing plant. While we may view such ingredients with revulsion, wild dogs will naturally devour bones, intestines and so on and the nutrients they contain form a valuable part of their diet. The difference is that wild meat is fresh and raw and hasn't been processed. Nor does it contain the type of chemicals that are regularly fed to intensively reared farm animals.
- Digest. Digest of meat or poultry is 'material' that has been recovered from carcasses using chemical enzymes. 'Material' should not be confused with meat.

Cereals. Corn, corn gluten, wheat and other cereals are frequently used in dog food as fillers, sweeteners and to supply some of the protein content more cheaply than meat. The problem with cereals, especially corn and wheat, is that they are not as easy for the dog to digest and can cause allergic reactions that show up in excessive licking and scratching, coughing and sneezing, or frequent ear infections. Corn can also cause bloating.

Oils and fats. The extreme heat and pressure of the rendering process separates fat from meat. But as we all know, fat is what makes meat more palatable – a steak lightly marbled with fat is juicier and tastier than an extra lean cut. Pet-food manufacturers realise this too, which is why fat is often sprayed onto the food at the end of processing. Good fats for dogs include poultry or chicken fat; less digestible fat sources are beef tallow or animal fat. Preservatives have to be added to the food to prevent the fats from spoiling.

Additives. Commercial dog foods contain a host of added ingredients, including colourings, preservatives and vitamins and minerals. On the face of it, we should be pleased to see vitamins and minerals listed on the packet. At last, here's some evidence that the food has health-giving properties. But vitamins and minerals are added to cheap dog food because processing has destroyed the nutrients that were present in the ingredients in the first place. The same goes for flavourings – what's lost in the processing has to be added in at the end. Dogs rarely turn their noses up at food if they are hungry – and some dogs never turn their noses up at food at all – but others require persuasion. Flavourings give dog food a meaty smell that reassures owners the food is wholesome. And food colouring is there for our benefit, too – dogs have poor colour vision.

More worrying are the chemicals that are added to dog food to give it a long shelf life. You will often see 'EC-permitted antioxidants, flavourings and colourings' on the label. These preservatives can include ethoxyquin and the antioxidants BHA (butylated hydroxyanisole) and BHT (butylated hydroxtoluene). A recent Japanese study showed that both BHA and BHT can cause various cancers, as well as liver and kidney dysfunction. Ethoxyquin, a chemical that is classified by the US Department of Agriculture as a toxic pesticide, is implicated in cancers of the stomach, bladder and kidney. Propylene glycol – a chemical often added to semi-moist dog food – is similar in composition to anti-freeze and has been shown to destroy red blood cells. Less drastic side effects of chemical preservatives include dry skin, allergies, dental problems and lack of energy. Other dogs react to preservatives by becoming hyperactive – just like kids who have had too many fizzy drinks.

The numbers game

To make proper comparisons between different types of dog food, and in particular between wet and dry varieties, you're going to need a bit of maths. Most nutritional recommendations for dogs are given on what's known as a *dry matter basis*. That means food with no water added. All pet foods contain moisture, even dry foods, so you need to do a conversion.

Manufacturers have to list ingredients by proportion, but only in the form the food is fed. Many canned dog foods, for example, contain up to 80 per cent moisture. If the label says that the food is 10 per cent protein, it would mean that if you took out all the water, half of what was left, that is the actual food itself, would be protein. Leaving aside the fact that this is an expensive way to buy water, you can see that the food the dog is getting has a very high protein content. And it may be even higher. It is not illegal to state that a food contains 10 per cent protein when the protein content is actually 15 per cent. On a dry matter basis, that's a lot of protein.

A further difficulty is that you won't exactly know what form that protein takes. Many of the cheaper brands of dog food contain too much protein and too much fat. Protein is the most expensive ingredient in dog food, so if the food costs peanuts, you'll know the protein isn't high quality. It may chiefly consist of cereal proteins, which are not easily digestible by dogs. Manufacturers often disguise a high cereal content by listing different forms of the same basic ingredient separately on the label. Corn, for example, might crop up several times in the ingredients as 'ground corn' or 'flaked corn' or 'corn gluten'. The label may lead you to believe you are feeding your dog a chicken-based dog food, when you are actually feeding him corn, which his system can't cope with.

Homemade dog food

Dissatisfaction with the shortcomings of commercial dog food has led some people to take matters into their own hands and make their own. The numbers aren't huge, but a fair few pet owners are swapping doggie recipes out there.

There are broadly two schools of thought. One approach is to feed dogs high-quality cooked human food and the other, often known as the BARF (Bones and Raw Food) diet, seeks to approximate the kind of diet a dog would have in the wild. Those who favour the cooked option argue that cooked food is safer and easier to digest. They also maintain that during the dog's long association with humans, his digestion has adapted to cope with the vegetables and cooked whole grains that, along with animal protein, formed the basis of the human diet before mass-produced foods came on the scene. Those who advocate feeding raw food believe that millions of years of evolution count for more than thousands of years of domestication. In other words, they argue that when dogs left the wilderness behind, they took their physiology with them.

Most vets (and, it goes without saying, pet-food companies) warn against homemade dog food on the grounds that it is difficult to make sure that a dog gets all the nutrients he needs. I think it's fair to say that if you adopt either approach, you're going to have to devote a good deal of time and effort into sourcing and preparing ingredients, weighing them out and making sure you get the proportions right. Ensuring that there is enough variety in the diet, whether it is raw or cooked, is key, which means you will need to be pretty clued up on nutrition. For example, vegetables can be a useful source of nutrients, especially carbohydrates, vitamins and minerals. But spinach and cauliflower are high in protein; adding these ingredients to a dog's diet that was already rich in protein might cause problems.

Cooking for dogs

A home-cooked meal doesn't mean pizza, burgers and chips, or any of the highly processed fast foods we eat so much of these days. Ingredients should be fresh, unadulterated and lightly cooked by poaching, blanching, or steaming to preserve as many nutrients as possible. Fried foods are terrible for dogs. Leftovers and table scraps are fine, providing you keep an eye on the nutritional content and provided what went on the plate was good healthy food in the first place. But what most people leave on their plates – gravy or sauce, fatty or gristly meat trimmings, and foods high in carbohydrate – contains too little protein and too much fat to form the basis of a dog's diet. Your dog is not a dustbin, however keen he may be to poke his nose in one!

Some experts who have successfully fed dogs home-cooked food recommend a diet composed of one-third meat (beef, lamb, chicken, fish), one-third cooked brown rice and one-third cooked root and green vegetables. Seaweed, dried and fresh, is added to provide essential vitamins and minerals. This diet, however, is not suitable for dogs with food intolerances or those with conditions that affect their digestion. You'll also need a knowledge of dog nutrition to ensure you steer clear of any ingredients that are indigestible or harmful to dogs, or that might cause problems with your particular breed. Dalmatians, for example, are predisposed to form stones in their urinary tracts if they eat too much of a type of protein known as a purine. Liver is high in purines and so are various other foods.

Your dog is not a dustbin, however keen he may be to poke his nose in one!

The BARF diet

More controversial than home-cooked dog food is the BARF (Bones and Raw Food) diet, where dogs are fed exclusively on raw food. A large proportion of that diet is raw meaty bones. Some owners swear passionately by this approach, but it is not without its critics.

The BARF diet (also known as Biologically Appropriate Raw Foods) recommends the following breakdown:

- 60 per cent raw meaty bones (including raw chicken bones)
- 15 per cent raw vegetables, crushed or pulped in a food processor or juicer
- 10 per cent raw offal (organ meats such as liver and kidney)
- 10 per cent supplementary foods such as oils, garlic, kelp, yoghurt and cottage cheese to provide healthy bacteria and other nutrients
- 5 per cent fruit (very ripe but not rotten)

Because of the dangers posed by raw meat these days, it is essential to obtain meat and bones from a supplier who can guarantee that they come from a good source. Unless your vegetables are organic, you must also wash them well to remove any traces of chemicals or pesticides. Pulping the vegetables reduces them to the state in which they would be found in the stomach of the dog's prey and makes them more digestible.

Advocates of the BARF diet, whose leading exponent is Dr Ian Billinghurst, an Australian vet, maintain that this diet, which contains little or no carbohydrate, is correct in an evolutionary sense and provides many health benefits, including better dental health and prevention of degenerative diseases. A particular feature of the diet is that food types are never combined, but fed separately. Feeding is also less frequent than in other regimes to mimic a wild dog's natural periods of fasting and feasting.

The central controversy of the diet concerns the issue of feeding dogs raw bones. Vets often advise against feeding dogs bones of any kind, raw or cooked, because of the risk that the bones may splinter or be swallowed whole and cause an obstruction in the intestinal tract.

Fans of 'natural' dog diets maintain that dogs have evolved to eat raw bones and that they deliver important health benefits. They say raw bones are a good source both of calcium and 'friendly' bacteria, help keep teeth and gums healthy, and prevent blockages of the anal glands. In contrast, they are totally opposed to feeding dogs cooked bones of any kind, as these are more brittle and lack the nutrients that are found in the raw marrow and fresh bone material.

If you do decide to feed your dog raw bones, the following precautions are recommended:

- The bones should be fresh or frozen and from a good source. Don't feed pork bones, which aren't readily digestible.
- Introduce bones slowly. Feed ground bone to begin with and watch the dog's stools for any digestive upset. Too much bone in the diet can also cause constipation.
- Feeding bones to dogs that are already on natural diets minimises the risks. Never feed raw bones to dogs with sensitive digestions, or dogs that are ill or that suffer from an impaired immune system.
- Large knuckle bones that dogs have to chew slowly are better than small bones that dogs can bolt whole. Keep raw chicken wings and other small bones out of the diet until your dog is used to eating bones.

It isn't within the scope of this book to describe the BARF diet in full detail, nor is it my intention to weigh in on one side of the argument or the other. If you are attracted by this approach, there are a number of publications available. But before making this type of radical change to your dog's diet, it is a good idea to consult your vet first to find out whether there is any aspect of your dog's health or his particular breed makeup that would make such a change unadvisable. (See also Changing your dog's diet, page 104.)

Vegetarian dogs

There are some owners who, for ethical reasons, want to feed their dogs a vegetarian diet. I have to say that I'm opposed to this. Dogs may be more omnivorous than cats but they still need the type of protein that is found in meat. A dog should not be made to suffer for his owner's beliefs.

Feeding times

Some people feed their dogs once a day; some three or even four times a day in line with human mealtimes. Then there are others who offer food round the clock, a practice that is known as 'free feeding'. In my experience, twice is about right for an adult, active dog that has no health problems. Feeding a dog only once a day can cause dramatic swings in blood sugar levels resulting in hyperactivity or lethargy, depending on whether it's just after chow time or just before it. It can also put a strain on the digestive tract so that the dog suffers from bloating. On the other hand, offering food more often than twice, especially free feeding, means that the dog's digestive system is always on the go, churning away, which can interfere with rest periods. For exceptions to these feeding intervals, see Chapter Two, page 58.

Mealtimes are undoubtedly the high points of a dog's day. Most dogs will anticipate the dinner hour with such accuracy you would think they could tell the time. Some of our smarter four-legged friends will try to beat the clock by asking for food a little earlier each day. In some cases, this might be the result of hunger or malnourishment. If a dog is not getting what he needs from his food, or it is passing too quickly through his system, he's going to be asking for more and more and more in an attempt to satisfy his hunger. The same is true if he's got an underlying condition, such as a digestive disorder, or a parasitic infection, which will affect his appetite. In other circumstances, begging for food can indicate that there isn't much else in the day for the dog to look forward to. Stepping up exercise and stimulation is the answer here. But if you can rule out these causes, then your dog is trying to train you to feed him on demand. And succeeding, if you give in!

As your dog's leader, you have to send out a clear message that you are in charge of the food. You can enhance your value in your dog's eyes by being in control of his food source at all times.

Here are some guidelines for mealtimes:

- Stick to set feeding times – once in the morning and once later on in the afternoon. When your dog sees that you are in control of his food, he will be more likely to listen to you because you are in charge of a resource that is particularly valuable to him.
- Fill your dog's bowl on the kitchen counter, not on the floor in front of him.
- Tell him to sit and stay until you have put the food on the floor. Then give him a release command.
- Allow a dog 20 minutes to finish his food. Most dogs will wolf down their food in a fraction of that time, but if he leaves food in his bowl after 20 minutes, take it away.
- Water must always be freely available.
- Don't attempt to train a dog right after meals. If he's a little hungry, he'll work harder for his rewards.

Mealtimes are undoubtedly the high points of a dog's day.

Feeding equipment

There are many types of bowls and feeding dishes on the market, in a range of materials including plastic, ceramic and metal. In general, the heavier and more stable containers are better than lightweight ones as they are not so easily nudged along the floor or tipped over while the dog is eating. Avoid plastic bowls as they tend to harbour bacteria even after they are washed.

Choose an appropriate size and always wash the bowl after feeding. Dirty bowls, encrusted with food residues, attract flies and are unhygienic. Make sure you keep the feeding area clean, too. You can put down washable plastic mats if your dog tends to be a messy eater. Make sure you keep dog bowls, dishes and the utensils you use to prepare or cook food separate from those you and your family use.

For breeds with long, floppy ears, such as spaniels, tall, narrow feeding dishes are better than shallow bowls. This ensures the ears fall outside the dish and are kept clean and free from food particles, which might encourage the ear infections to which these breeds can be prone. Really large breeds such as Great Danes may find it more comfortable to eat if their dish is raised a little off the ground. The same is true for older dogs that may be getting a little stiff in their joints.

My space

Give some thought to where you feed your dog. Dogs are particularly sensitive to their immediate environment at chow time. A dog that feels vulnerable or stressed may be more likely to bolt his food or go off it completely. Give him plenty of space away from busy areas where people and other pets are coming and going all the time.

Eating between meals: snacks and treats

Most dogs are highly food-oriented and will work hard for a treat. For this reason, food treats are indispensable in training, especially as a top reward or 'bonus' treat. The trouble with many mass-produced dog treats, however, is that they are no better for your dog than mass-produced dog food. Pet foods marketed as dog 'snacks' or 'treats' are not required to include nutritional information on the packet – and if they don't tell you what's in them, you can guess what that means!

It's easy to make your own dog treats. I give strips of cooked chicken, beef and liver as rewards during my training sessions.

I also give pieces of raw carrot and apple (but not apple seeds which can be poisonous for dogs). Rawhide chews should only be given to dogs under supervision. The softened fragments can sometimes cause choking, while some dogs may suffer from upset stomachs and loose stools. Don't give rawhide chews to puppies.

Too much snacking between meals can be just as bad for dogs as it is for humans. Too many high-fat treats between meals can be a cause of pancreatitis in dogs. I don't mean a few chicken strips given during a training session, but more substantial treats handed out round the clock. Keep an eye on quantity as much as quality.

Quantities

How much should you feed your dog? That's the \$64,000 question and it's almost unanswerable in general terms. Enough, but not too much. Enough to keep him active and maintain his weight within the recommended range for his breed. Enough for his particular stage in life.

Large dogs obviously need more food than small ones. Dogs that are very active, generally those whose ancestors were working breeds, need more calories than dogs bred chiefly for human companionship. Snoozing on a lap doesn't take much energy, after all.

Many commercial dog foods come with recommendations regarding quantities printed on the packaging. But as it is in the manufacturer's interest to sell you more dog food, you can't rely entirely on these.

One indication that you're feeding your dog too much is if he leaves food in his bowl. But this is not an infallible guide. Some dogs are so food-oriented that they will eat whatever is put in front of them, and then some. These include breeds such as retrievers and spaniels, which are notorious for putting on excess weight given any opportunity. Leaving food is also a warning sign of illness or some other disorder, particularly if your dog has always shown a healthy appetite before. On the other hand, you can't necessarily assume that just because your dog devours what is put in front of him and begs for more that you aren't offering enough. As I've previously mentioned, it could be hunger, it could be malnourishment, it could be a parasitic infection, or it could be plain old boredom.

I always advise people to consult their vet for basic guidelines about how much to feed their dog. That's the first step. After that, it's a question of monitoring his condition. If he's a purebred animal, it's easy to determine what is the ideal weight range for his breed by consulting a chart. Weigh him regularly, or have him weighed at the vet's, and if he stays within the range and is alert and active, he's getting what he needs. If he's losing weight or underweight, you need to step up the calories. And if he's overweight, he needs less food and more exercise. Crossbreeds and mongrels don't feature on breed charts. That doesn't matter because there's a simple rule of thumb that applies to all dogs. If a dog is the right weight you should be able to feel his ribs clearly under his coat but you should not be able to see them.

What to avoid

There are a number of human foods you should never feed a dog. Most of these are common-sense no-no's, but others are less familiar. As dogs are natural scavengers, they sometimes eat positively harmful substances and give themselves a bad case of poisoning. Prevention is the only way. Dog-proof your house and garden the way you would for a baby or toddler and keep potentially lethal substances locked away, including alcohol, household chemicals and medicines.

Chocolate

Chocolate can kill dogs, especially baking or plain chocolate that contains a greater proportion of cocoa solids, but in sufficient quantities milk chocolate can also be harmful. (Incidentally, chocolate is also toxic for cats.) The two chemicals that cause the damage are caffeine and theobromine, but it is theobromine that is the more lethal. Caffeine acts on a dog in much the same way as it does on humans, but because dogs are smaller, the effect is exaggerated. Caffeine has a direct effect on the central nervous system and signs of overdose include extreme jumpiness and sensitivity to noise. Theobromine is found in higher concentrations in unsweetened chocolate and cocoa powder. A single ounce, or 25g, of unsweetened chocolate can kill a 10lb/4.5kg dog. In the case of milk chocolate, the lethal dose is 11oz/350g for a dog of the same size. Theobromine overstimulates the heart and can lead to seizures and coma. Signs of overdose include restlessness, thirst, vomiting, diarrhoea, irregular heartbeat, excessive urination and muscle tremors. These symptoms rarely show up immediately, but generally come on a few hours after the chocolate has been eaten. If you suspect your dog has eaten chocolate, get him to the vet straight away – and keep your chocolate treats well out of harm's way, and that includes chocolate cake.

Chicken bones

Most people are aware of the risk poultry bones pose for dogs – except, it seems, all those thoughtless individuals who scatter the remains of their fast food all over the pavement. Poultry bones – the bones of chickens, turkeys and game – are very brittle and splintery when they're cooked, and it's easy for dogs to choke on the fragments or for sharp splinters to pierce the intestine or abdominal wall, in which case infection often follows. Lamb chop bones can also be hazardous in this respect.

Onions

Onions in any form – raw, cooked or dried – are toxic for dogs. A chemical found in onions causes a dog's red blood cells to weaken and rupture, which in turn leads to anaemia. The more onion a dog eats, the more serious the effect. Signs of onion toxicity generally appear several days after the onion was eaten. Garlic, a natural antibiotic and some say a flea-repellent, is safe for dogs in moderation.

Raisins and grapes

An increasing number of cases have been seen of raisin and grape poisoning in dogs. From available evidence, as little as seven raisins or grapes can be toxic. If you suspect your dog has eaten raisins or grapes, get him to the vet straight away. Signs of toxicity include vomiting, food refusal, diarrhoea and lethargy. Untreated, a dog will develop acute kidney (renal) failure and die.

Sweets

Cakes, sweets and biscuits should never be fed to dogs. They contain too much refined sugar and a high proportion of fat. Keep your human treats well away from dogs. If you give your dog a small plain biscuit or a slice of buttered toast you are giving him the equivalent of a hamburger in human terms.

Cat food

Cats have different nutritional needs than dogs. They require more protein and more fat in their diets, which makes their food unsuitable for dogs (and vice versa). Feed pets separately and make sure your cat's food is out of your dog's reach.

Garden hazards

Gardens and parks often pose a risk for dogs. As far as plants are concerned, the danger list includes holly and mistletoe berries; yew, box and laurel leaves; rhododendron, hydrangea, columbine, lily of the valley and ivy, as well as spring flower bulbs, and sweet pea, wisteria and bluebell seeds. All of these are poisonous to dogs. Keep all pesticides, fertilisers, rat poisons and house or garden chemicals locked away.

Puddles

Dogs often make a beeline for puddles or water that has been sitting around for a while, for example in a watering can. Don't let your dog drink from puddles in the street. They may contain antifreeze, which has a sweet taste that appeals to dogs, but which can be fatal even in small doses.

Bright eyes and bushy tails

Feeding your dog a balanced diet that includes all the right nutrients in a properly digestible form will show up very obviously in his general condition. A healthy dog looks healthy. And he acts healthy, too – alert, active, eager for exercise and play.

And because what goes in comes out, you can also tell if what your dog is eating is upsetting his digestion by looking at his stools. Frequent, loose, smelly stools can indicate that the food is rushing through his system without the nutrients being properly absorbed. Diarrhoea and vomiting can be a sign of food intolerance (as well as many other conditions). A dog fed the right diet will have well-formed and compacted brown stools and will pass these without straining.

Really serious signs of ill health will send most responsible pet owners straight to the vet's. Does it matter if your dog is scratching or shedding, or if his teeth aren't pearly white? Does it matter if he smells a little? Some experts believe these signs can be early warnings of diseases and disorders that come on in later life, seemingly out of the blue. Many are preventable with good diet and proper exercise.

Signs of good health:

- Bright, clear eyes that are free from discharge
- Cold, damp nose, with no significant discharge. (A little clear fluid is OK.)
- Clean ears, with no unpleasant odour or visible wax
- Shiny coat
- Clear skin without dry or irritated patches
- Firm, well-muscled body
- White, smooth teeth
- Pleasant smelling breath

Smile please!

Tartar is a hard, yellow substance that accumulates around the base of teeth and damages the gums. In time, bacteria gets into tooth sockets and teeth eventually loosen and fall out. A dog that has poor dental health will have yellow teeth, red inflamed gums and bad breath. Dry food does not prevent dental problems, contrary to popular belief. Raw food, especially meat, can help and nylon dental bones are also good. The best option is to clean your dog's teeth once a day with a soft toothbrush or canine dental aid. Use a saltwater solution or dog toothpaste.

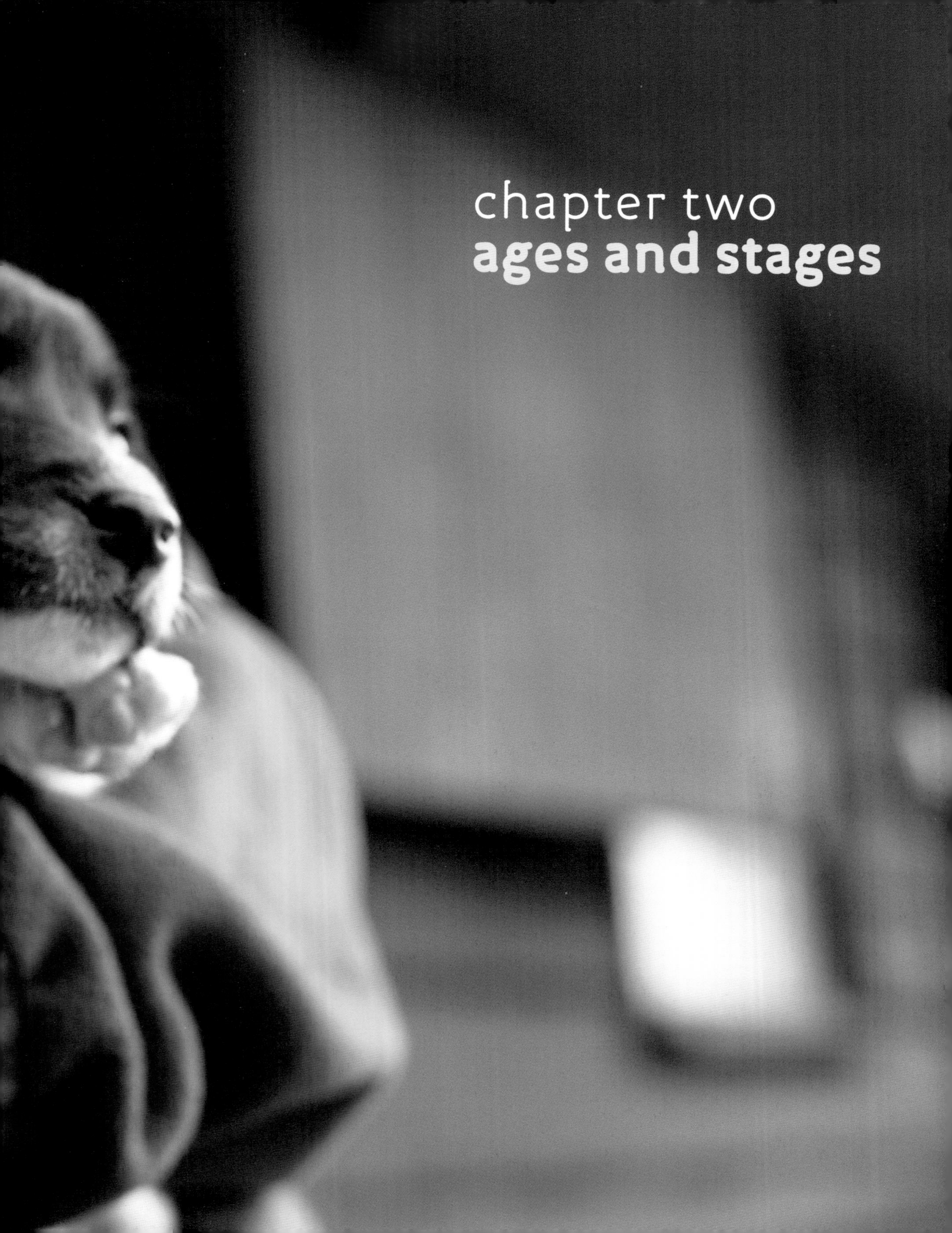

chapter two
ages and stages

In this chapter I'll be looking at some of the variables that can have a bearing on what you give your dog to eat. The most obvious of these is age. Growing puppies need a different proportion of nutrients than adult dogs and more frequent feeding. Older dogs, that are slowing down, need a little extra in their diets to help bolster their immune systems and keep them healthy for longer.

Similar adjustments must be made to accommodate periods when a female dog is pregnant or lactating, or to help a sick dog convalesce. Levels of activity are another key variable, which can affect not only how much you feed your dog, but also the nutritional composition of that food.

Then there are breed variations. The domestic dog is an incredibly varied species, ranging from fluffy little toy poodles to giant mastiffs. While selective breeding has given humans companions and workmates uniquely suited to their different roles, it has also made some breeds more susceptible to certain illnesses than others. Some of these have dietary triggers.

Nutritionists talk about growth, ageing, pregnancy and lactation as 'stress' periods for dogs. What they mean in simple terms is that the body is under a certain amount of pressure due to metabolic changes. But dogs that are fed incorrectly at any stage of life will also experience stress, which tends to show up first in the weakest part of the body, often the skin and the coat, but sometimes in the digestive tract.

Like the young of any species, puppies have special nutritional requirements. It takes a year for most pups to reach an adult size and level of development and growth is particularly rapid in the early weeks and months. When puppies are very small, their stomachs are tiny, so they need more frequent feeding than adult dogs.

Before birth

Puppies get the best possible start in life if they come from healthy parents that have been fed high-quality diets. A female also needs extra nutrients during pregnancy and lactation to produce vigorous puppies with strong immune systems.

For the first six weeks of pregnancy, a maintenance diet is adequate for the mum-to-be. During the last two to three weeks, however, she needs a diet that is slightly higher in protein and one that contains more calories. As her belly swells she will find it easier to manage smaller, more frequent meals. Warming and moistening the food will help to encourage her to eat if she is reluctant. A sure sign that the big day is near is a sudden food refusal in the ninth week of pregnancy. Birth usually follows a day or two later.

The early weeks

Newborn pups are blind. But they do have a sense of smell, although it is not yet fully developed. After a pup is born, the mother will lay a saliva trail by licking the pup and then licking her teats so that he can find his way to his food. The more dominant individual in a litter will latch on to the front teat where the milk supply is richer, leaving the hind teats to his shyer and less outgoing brothers and sisters. In doing so, he gives himself a good head start in life and nature ensures the survival of the fittest genes. Breeders and owners can redress the balance a little, however, by helping a pup that has been crowded out to reach a nipple.

For the first three weeks, pups get all they need from their mother's milk, including the important antibodies and nutrients in the 'first milk' or colostrum. One of these nutrients is Vitamin A. Puppies are born with no Vitamin A stored in their livers and the Vitamin A in colostrum is vital for their healthy development.

Milk production is draining on the female dog's system. To produce a good supply of milk, a nursing dam needs up to three or four times her usual food intake at the peak of lactation, along with much more water. In general, it's recommended that you give her as much as she wants of both water and food in the first four weeks after birth. Many dams are reluctant to leave their puppies, so it's best to keep feeding and water dishes near the litter. You may also have to encourage her to eat. If you are offering her dry food, moisten it with water during this period, which will make it more palatable. It's not unusual for a puppy's first taste of solid food to come from his mother's bowl, which is another reason for making sure the food is moist.

Weight gain

A healthy puppy will gain weight from day one and carry on gaining until he has reached his adult size, which generally happens around the end of the first year. The faster growth period is in the first few months. At four months most dogs weigh half their adult weight and the weight gain then slows down. Giant breeds, however, do not reach their adult weight until they are almost two years old and the rate of growth doesn't begin to slow until 18 months. As a rough guide, puppies should gain ⅛oz/2–4g a day per 2lb/1kg of the recommended adult weight for their breed.

Puppies should be weighed regularly to ensure they are growing at the right rate – not too slowly, but not too fast, either. Before weaning, puppies that are not thriving may not be getting enough milk and may have to be fed a puppy supplement.

Weaning

Weaning is a gradual process in pups as it is in humans; the difference is that it happens a lot sooner. The mother's milk supply may start to dry up when the pups are about five to six weeks old, although some mothers lactate for longer. A couple of weeks before then is the time to begin to introduce new foods to the puppies – tastes at first, gradually increasing to small frequent meals. Sometimes lactose-free puppy replacement milk (available from veterinarians) is also fed during this transition time, mixed into puppy food to make a gruel. Pups should NEVER be fed cow's milk. Many breeds are lactose-intolerant and feeding cow's milk can cause allergic reactions and diarrhoea.

As the puppies gradually begin to eat more solid food, you should reduce their mother's intake until it is only one and a half times what it would be normally. A reputable breeder will only be prepared to part with a puppy once he is eight or nine weeks old. By that time he will not only be fully weaned but will have learned key social skills from his mother and littermates and will be mature enough to leave them without excessive stress.

Feeding your new puppy

Now it's up to you. Once you have brought your puppy home, he is entirely dependent on you for his wellbeing, health and happiness. Responsible breeders generally supply new dog owners with a diet sheet and sample of the food the puppy has been eating so that the feeding regime can proceed uninterrupted. If you disagree with what the puppy has been fed, don't change his diet straight away. Give him time to settle in his new environment and introduce your preferred food gradually over a period of a couple of weeks. Hopefully, however, you will be on the same wavelength as the breeder and feeding can proceed without drastic change.

Expect your new puppy to take a day or two to settle into a feeding pattern. He's coping with change on many fronts and this may affect his appetite. Don't rush to feed him as soon as you get him home. He'll have been used to eating with his littermates and may bolt down his food and give himself a stomach upset. Put water out but wait until he has settled a little to offer the first meal.

What makes the right diet for puppies is no less controversial than what's the correct food for adult dogs. Advocates of the 'natural' raw food diet may give raw 'whole animal' patties containing ground bone and supplement with pulped vegetables and tripe. (In some parts of the world these foods can be obtained ready prepared from specialist suppliers.) Or they may start as they mean to go on and offer raw chicken wings, along with other foods recommended by this approach. Those who cook for their dogs might give their pups a variety of soft foods, such as mince, scrambled egg and oat porridge. Most manufacturers of commercial dog food also produce special puppy foods. Like the adult dog products, these range from highly nutritious and digestible foods to the downright harmful.

My preference is to feed puppies the same kind of high-quality, hypoallergenic natural product I feed adult dogs, but in a 'growth' or 'puppy' formulation. These formulas contain more protein than adult or maintenance diets, which puppies need to build muscle and bone. They also contain the required level of vitamins and minerals for growth, which might otherwise be missing if you were to follow the cooked food approach. Supplementation is not needed if you feed a high-quality food and may even be harmful. At this stage, the food I offer puppies is chiefly wet, perhaps with a little dry food mixed in, as it is easier to digest, and I usually wait a while before introducing cooked chicken and vegetables. And, of course, fresh clean water must be available at all times.

Aside from the cooked versus raw food debate and the advisability or otherwise of feeding young dogs raw bones (see page 44), there is considerable disagreement about how much protein and fat puppies need in their diets. Some people claim that feeding too much protein and fat to puppies causes severe

problems in later life, including skeletal abnormalities and obesity. While a puppy does need more protein relative to his size than an adult dog, some of the cheaper puppy foods contain vast amounts of protein, often in a cereal form that is not properly digestible. It's not simply a question of too much protein in such cases, it's a question of the wrong kind of protein altogether. Puppies fed the wrong food may fail to thrive, or they may grow much too fast, or present early signs of dietary intolerance. At the very least, problems will be stored up for later.

Keep an eye on your puppy's growth and tailor the amounts you give him accordingly. In the old days people used to admire chubby babies. Now we are better clued up about nutrition we recognise that a fat baby is not necessarily a healthy one. The same shift has occurred in our perception of puppies. A plump pup is not the ideal. Leaner puppies who are building solid muscle at a slow and steady rate are much more likely to lead healthy lives.

Feeding large- and giant-breed puppies

Some of the large and giant breeds are prone to bone growth diseases. For example, hip dysplasia, an inherited condition that can cripple dogs or lead to arthritis in later life, also affects many breeds, including German shepherds, Labradors and other retrievers. Some experts believe that such disorders are purely genetic; others think that diet can have an important bearing on the severity or otherwise of the symptoms. Many pet-food companies now produce puppy food specifically for large and giant breeds. These contain lower amounts of protein so that puppies do not grow too fast – accelerated growth has been linked to these types of skeletal problems. As ever, READ the label.

Feeding times

Small meals about three or four times a day is about right for young puppies. By the time your puppy is five or six months old you can reduce the feeding time to two meals a day.

How you feed your pup is just as important as how often and how much. I don't start off feeding a puppy the way I would feed an adult dog. Instead, I take the opportunity to teach him that I am his food source and not a threat. I go out of my way to make mealtimes lovely occasions! This kind of positive training can help to avoid problems such as food guarding, when a dog can nip or lash out if anyone comes too close to his bowl.

Here's what to do:

- Choose a place where the puppy will not be distracted or feel threatened by people or other pets. Put an empty bowl on the floor.
- Get some puppy food – or a few pieces of cooked chicken – and sit beside the empty bowl.
- Now drop a little food into the bowl. Most puppies will make a beeline for it.
- While the puppy eats, keep adding food to the bowl, a little at a time.
- After a few sessions, you can fill your puppy's bowl on the counter and ask him to sit for it as you would do an adult dog. But carry on dropping the odd bit of food into the bowl from time to time to reinforce the message.

Chewing

Most dogs like to chew. It's natural behaviour. Chewing or gnawing on bones is how wild dogs gain important nutrients. In the process, the teeth are cleaned and the jaw muscles are exercised. Chewing is also a pacifying behaviour for some dogs. It releases all those happy chemicals in the brain. In other words, it's soothing.

Puppies need to chew for another reason and that is because they are teething. There are two acute phases of teething. The first is when the baby teeth are lost and the second, at about six to nine months of age, is when the adult teeth settle into the jawbone.

When we bring dogs into our human world, it's up to us to manage that environment for them. You can't stop a puppy from chewing and you shouldn't even try, but you can direct him to things that are good to chew and keep him away from what's harmful or destructive. Puppies in the throes of teething will chew on anything – designer shoes, table legs, skirting boards. They'll bite through flexes and wires given half the chance. Protect your puppy – and your home – just as you would a toddler in the try-anything daredevil stage. Use a baby gate to keep him in a safe area. Hard rubber toys, nylon bones and other virtually indestructible dog toys are good things for a puppy to chew. Whatever can easily be ripped up and ingested should be avoided.

Points to consider:

- Remember that some dogs chew excessively as a way of relieving boredom and anxiety. Anything to brighten the day! Dogs need company, attention and mental stimulation. They're social creatures – they're not equipped to spend long hours alone with nothing to do.
- Chewing in an older dog can also be a sign of painful teeth. Make sure you inspect your dog's teeth regularly – watch out for broken or chipped teeth, red gums and inflammation.

The older dog

Dogs, like people, are living longer these days. In the wild a dog rarely lives longer than five or six years. Our pets, sheltered from the elements and protected from all the hazards of living rough, generally live much longer than this. As veterinary science progresses and more people become aware of the importance of a healthy diet in the prevention of disease, that happy trend looks set to continue.

People used to feed their dogs the same food for their entire lives. But older dogs, or 'seniors', also have their own marketing niche. Many companies produce ranges specifically formulated for the pet that is getting on in years. A common problem of this stage in life is obesity. As the dog's activity level diminishes, he will be inclined to put on weight if the diet is not adjusted. Then it becomes a vicious circle, as the extra pounds place stresses on the dog's body, which, in turn, make him even less active. It is at this stage, too, that many serious diseases and disorders are more likely to show up, particularly in dogs that have been given an inadequate diet for years.

The ageing process

First things first. How old is old?

Most people are familiar with the saying that one year of a dog's life is equal to seven in human terms. That's no longer regarded as a reliable guide. Recent studies show that a ratio worked out by a French vet, Dr A LeBeau, is far more accurate. After all, a dog will have reached sexual maturity by the end of his first year, which is certainly not true of a seven-year-old child. LeBeau's ratio suggests that the first year of a dog's life is equivalent to 15 human years; the second to 24 human years and that each year after that equates to four human years. Here's how it looks:

Age of dog	Age of human
3 months	5 years
6 months	10 years
1 year	15 years
2 years	24 years
3 years	28 years
4 years	32 years
5 years	36 years
6 years	40 years
7 years	44 years
8 years	48 years
9 years	52 years
10 years	56 years
11 years	60 years
12 years	64 years
13 years	68 years
14 years	72 years
15 years	76 years
20 years	96 years

But we also know that different breeds age in different ways. Giant breeds such as Great Danes rarely live more than nine years or so, and are 'old' at six or seven. Large heavy dogs such as Rottweilers may make it into their early teens. It's the small- to medium-sized mongrels and cross-breeds that stand the best chance of enjoying a ripe old age, with some surviving until their late teens. Dogs are defined as 'old' when they have reached the last quarter of their expected lifespan. Size has an important bearing on the age at which dogs become 'seniors':

Senior age	Size
12 years	Small breeds or dogs weighing less than 20lb/9kg
10 years	Medium breeds or dogs weighing 21–50lb/9.5–22.7kg
9 years	Large dogs or dogs weighing 51–90lb/23–41kg
7 years	Giant breeds or dogs weighing over 90lb/41kg

The senior diet

No dog can live for ever. But diet plays a vital role in keeping a dog healthy for longer and bolstering his immune system so that he can fight off disease. If disease is already present in the older dog, the right diet can also help to manage the condition.

If you are choosing a commercial food for your older dog, it's important to read the fine print on the pet-food label. Many commercial foods for 'seniors' have lower levels of protein to reduce strain on the kidneys – kidney or renal failure is a common cause of death in older dogs. Some experts maintain, however, that protein levels are not implicated in the progression of kidney disease at all. What is certainly true is that the wrong type of protein, such as those cereal-based proteins many cheap commercial pet foods have in abundance, are very harmful to all dogs. An older dog needs protein to maintain muscle mass and at this stage of life it is even more important that the protein should be high quality, meat-based and easily digestible.

What an older dog undoubtedly needs is fewer calories. Even dogs that remain sprightly in their older years and enjoy regular exercise can put on weight due to metabolic change. A diet that is reduced in calories can help to keep the weight gain associated with ageing in check. It is also important to avoid any foods that contain added salt, which can put a strain on the heart.

Higher levels of key vitamins, minerals and fatty acids have been shown to benefit the older dog. GLA (gamma-linolenic acid) is an omega-6 fatty acid that helps keep a dog's skin and coat healthy. Dogs fed the right diet normally produce GLA in their livers, but levels often drop with age. Antioxidants also play an important role in maintaining a healthy immune system and destroy dangerous 'free radicals', molecules that accelerate ageing and cause diseases such as cancer. A good 'senior' food should include GLA and have higher levels of antioxidants such as Vitamin E and beta-carotene.

Points to consider:

- Check your older dog's teeth regularly for signs of decay and gum inflammation. A dog with a sore mouth will find it difficult to eat. Brush your dog's teeth, give him a dental bone to chew, or feed hard, raw food such as carrots and apples to prevent the build-up of tartar.
- Watch your dog's weight. Although most older dogs have a tendency to gain weight, some will lose it. If your dog has lost weight, take him to the vet for a check-up to make sure there is no medical cause. A distended stomach can be an indication that the heart and lungs are not working effectively, causing a build-up of fluid.
- A sign of failing kidneys is increased thirst and reduced appetite.
- It's sometimes a good idea to feed older dogs smaller portions more often – three to four times a day. This eases the strain on their digestion.

- Older dogs may have impaired senses of smell and taste, which reduces their appetite. Frequent feeding and warming food to increase palatability can help.
- If your dog is getting stiff in his joints or has trouble bending down, raise his feeding bowl so he can reach it easily.
- Stick to a consistent daily routine to keep your dog's stress levels down. Dramatic changes to his environment or routine should be avoided as far as possible. Bringing a new puppy into the home can sometimes give an older but otherwise healthy dog a new lease of life if the introduction is gradual and properly managed. Sometimes, however, it can be a real shock to the system, and that's not fair on your old dog or your new puppy.

Working dogs

One of the reasons why it is difficult to give hard and fast rules about the amount you should feed your dog is that dogs do vary a great deal in their levels of activity. Of course, some dogs have lazy owners and the reason why their exercise periods are short and infrequent has nothing to do with their general breed disposition. Given half the chance, these poor pooches would clip on their own leads and drag their humans out to the park with them! Nevertheless, there is a great difference between the natural activity level of a Border collie, bred to herd sheep on hillsides all day long, and a toy breed like the cavalier King Charles spaniel, which is foremost a companion animal.

All dogs need regular exercise, including walks, free-running off the lead and periods of play, and I'll be talking about these in later chapters. Most pet dogs require about the same 'maintenance' diet once they have reached adulthood, in quantities that are appropriate to their size and basic level of activity. If your dog is a working or performance dog, however, you will need to adjust the diet to give him the extra fuel he needs. It's not simply a question of giving him more – the balance of nutrients may also require fine-tuning.

Working dogs – herders, sled dogs and hunting dogs – as well as dogs involved in intense physical training need a diet with a high nutrient density. This generally translates as about 26 per cent protein (as opposed to the 20 per cent provided by a maintenance diet), 10 per cent fat and 30 per cent carbohydrate, which will give a higher calorific content. This high-energy food should only be given during the dog's working or training periods. When the working or training season is over, he will need to go back to a maintenance diet.

If you've got a working or performance dog, don't feed him immediately before or after a period of exertion. You can keep him going while he's out and about with small treats and fresh water, but restrict the main feeding times to quieter rest periods.

Rescue dogs

I've nurtured a lot of rescue dogs in my time and they come into my home from all sorts of backgrounds. Some of them are in poor condition when they arrive; others are physically OK but have suffered other kinds of neglect. Quite frequently, the dog's past experiences will show up in eating behaviour.

When I bring a rescue dog home for the first time, I don't offer him food right away. I let him get used to the sights, sounds and smells of his new environment for about an hour or so and then I take him out for a bit of a walk. After that, I offer some food.

Many rescue dogs are food bolters. You set the dish on the floor and the food's gone in seconds. One obvious reason is hunger – after all, when a rescue dog arrives in your home he may not have eaten for days. Bolting or wolfing down food can also be a sign that the dog has survived by scavenging. Scavengers have to be quick and they often have to fight for their spoils. If the dog has been living in an environment where there's not much food around or where food is associated with threat, discomfort or stress, he'll be more likely to seize his chance and eat it as fast as possible. Take the opportunity to make eating times as comfortable and happy as you can. Make sure the eating area is a stress-free zone. You can also use the techniques described on pages 128 if your dog is over-protective of his food and growls or snaps if anyone approaches his bowl.

Some rescue dogs are just too stressed to eat at all for the first few days. Don't panic and don't press food on them. Make sure water is available at all times and do all you can to reassure the dog that his new home is a safe and happy place. Once he has begun to settle a little, you can entice him to eat by warming the food a little and sprinkling a little chopped garlic on top. Warming food releases the scent molecules and makes the food more appetising to the dog. Most dogs also find garlic very appealing.

Convalescing dogs

Illness or major medical interventions such as surgery place enormous stress on the dog's body. The dog may have lost important nutrients through gastrointestinal upset or suffered trauma of some kind. Always consult your vet about the correct diet to feed a dog recovering from a particular illness or an operation.

Some conditions naturally affect the dog's appetite. But to make a good recovery and build up his strength, he's going to need food that is both easily digestible and that has increased nutrient content. Healing and recovery requires extra energy.

When I am nursing a sick dog back to health I generally give him what most vets recommend, which is a bland, easily digested diet of cooked chicken and rice. I warm the food very slightly to make it more palatable. This is also a good recovery food if the dog has had a bout of diarrhoea or an upset stomach of some kind. Once your dog is showing signs of alertness, increased activity and is generally returning to his usual perky self, you can gradually reintroduce his normal food.

Chronic digestive diseases

Diseases such as diabetes and pancreatitis are showing up more frequently in dogs these days. Many people believe that the higher incidence of these digestive conditions is linked to inadequate nutrition.

Both diabetes and pancreatitis are conditions that affect the pancreas, the organ in the body responsible for producing the hormone insulin, which controls sugar levels in the blood. Diet plays a large part in managing these conditions. Always seek veterinary advice about feeding regimes.

Diabetes mellitus

Symptoms include:

- Excessive drinking, eating and increased frequency of urination
- Weight loss or gain
- The sudden onset of cataracts in the eyes
- Occasionally vomiting and lack of energy.

Diabetic dogs need daily injections of insulin and a strictly regulated diet. Exercise must also be consistent – the same amount at the same times of day – to keep blood sugar levels as steady as possible. Switching to a high-fibre, low-carbohydrate diet that contains a high-quality protein is also advised. Feeding times must also be consistent.

Pancreatitis

In addition to producing insulin, the pancreas also secretes enzymes to aid digestion. In pancreatitis, it is the enzyme-producing portion of the pancreas that is inflamed and damaged. One of the triggers is a diet too rich in fat. Some breeds, notably miniature schnauzers and some spaniels, are more susceptible than others. Often these are dogs that are naturally 'greedier' or food-oriented and more likely to scavenge. A single blow-out on chicken skin from the rubbish bin can trigger a life-threatening episode in some animals. Other dogs present with a mild form of the condition.

Acute pancreatitis is a medical emergency. Symptoms include:

- Fever
- Restlessness due to pain – the abdomen will be tight
- Vomiting, diarrhoea and food refusal
- Dehydration
- Jaundice, which is often most obvious in the urine – it will be bright yellow.

Immediate treatment, usually in hospital, is necessary. At the beginning, fluids are given intravenously, along with pain relief and anti-nausea medication. As the dog improves, water and low-fat foods are introduced.

A dog that has suffered an attack of acute pancreatitis will probably have to be fed a low-fat diet for the rest of his life. Prescription foods are available that contain a low percentage of fat and fibre and which are highly digestible. Mild forms of the condition are harder to diagnose, but are treated in the same way.

Breed variations

The selective breeding of dogs has been great – for humans. Over the centuries we've created an incredibly varied species that meets our aesthetic preferences and practical requirements for domestic and working companions. But it's been more of a mixed blessing for dogs. Encouraging certain characteristics at the expense of others through breeding can predispose some dogs to health problems. Dachshunds, for example, bred to go to earth and flush out badgers from their sets, have very short legs for the size of their bodies and this can lead to lameness in later life. Genetic problems such as hip dysplasia also tend to show up more in certain breeds. Dietary intolerance is another area that can be breed-specific.

Just because a certain breed is predisposed to a particular dietary intolerance does not mean every individual animal will suffer in this way. Diagnostic tests can be carried out in some cases. But it is often better to be safe than sorry and keep the foods that might trigger problems out of the diet altogether.

It's beyond the scope of this book to provide an exhaustive guide as to how diet affects different breeds. It is always advisable to do your research and find out as much as you can about your dog's particular breed, so you are forewarned and forearmed.

Selective breeding can predispose some dogs to health problems.

German shepherds

German shepherds often suffer from a condition known as pancreatic insufficiency, in which the pancreas does not produce enough dietary enzymes. In fact, 70 per cent of dogs that have this condition are German shepherds. Affected dogs cannot digest their food properly and become malnourished as a result. Symptoms include weight loss, poor condition, ravenous appetite and rancid, foamy stools. The treatment involves supplementing the dog's food with enzymes in powder or pill form and changing to a diet that is low in fat, with an easily digestible carbohydrate and high-quality protein content. Feeding this type of diet from an early age may slow the progress of the condition.

West Highland terriers

Skin irritation and eczema are common in this breed. Dietary intolerances often show up in skin problems, as do allergies. Essential fatty acids are particularly beneficial in keeping skin healthy; feeding a high-quality, hypoallergenic, organic diet can alleviate symptoms. Supplements of omega fatty acids can also help.

Golden retrievers

Normally a gentle and affectionate dog, some Goldens suffer from a condition known as hepatic encephalopathy that can cause symptoms similar to a migraine in a human. Just after feeding, the dog may become irritable and aggressive, returning to normal some while later. In affected dogs, blood that would normally be filtered of toxins in the liver enters the general circulation and affects brain function. Symptoms vary widely from involuntary movements and behavioural changes to stunted growth, vomiting and seizures. Foods that are high in protein, in particular the wrong kind of protein, can make the condition worse. A high-quality, low-protein diet is advised, along with medical help.

Dalmatians

Dalmatians have special dietary requirements because they are predisposed to form stones in the urinary tract that can block urine flow completely. The trigger for stone-formation has been shown to be a particular type of protein called a purine. The answer is not a low-protein diet, but a diet with a low purine content. Foods high in purines include organ meats and beef, along with spinach, asparagus, cauliflower and lentils. Liver is one of the worst offenders and must never be offered, not even as a treat. Lamb and poultry have a lower purine content. Eggs, fruit and most vegetables excluding those mentioned above are very low in purines.

chapter three

fat dogs and problem eaters

Obesity is one of the biggest problems facing our pets today. It has been estimated that 40 per cent of our dogs are overweight and a shocking 25 per cent are obese. Some experts put the figures even higher. But one thing is clear. If your dog is fat, it's not his fault. It's yours.

Owners who feed their pets too much, or give them food that is inappropriate, are killing their dogs with kindness. Of course, dogs also become overweight when they aren't exercised enough – the correct level of activity is an important part of the equation. In this chapter, however, I'm going to focus on diet and how you can help your dog regain the lean muscled physique that is the sign of peak health and fitness. Canine weight-watchers, anybody?

It has to be said that some breeds are more predisposed to put on weight than others. These include Labradors, cocker spaniels, Shetland sheepdogs, beagles, basset hounds, pugs and dachshunds. But that's no excuse for letting your dog become obese. If you own one of these dogs, you need to take extra care over your dog's diet and exercise regime. Owners of whippets, greyhounds, borzois and salukis – breeds that are naturally lean – have less of a struggle because nature is on their side.

It is worth pointing out that a dog can become overweight not simply through overfeeding, but if he is receiving the wrong balance of nutrients in his diet. All dogs on any kind of diet, good, bad and indifferent, will gain weight if they are fed too much. But feeding a dog a poor-quality dog food that contains too much fat and sweeteners to make it palatable can also pile on the pounds. And it's not just what's in the dog bowl. Treats of inappropriate human food or cheap commercial dog treats can be calorie bombs. Dogs fed poor diets can be both overweight and malnourished.

Before you go ahead and put your dog on a weight-reducing programme, or change his brand of food to a healthier option, it is always advisable to consult your vet. Many owners only take their dogs to the vet for the yearly check-up and vaccinations, or when there is a clear sign of illness. But vets have an important role to play in preventative medicine, too. Maintaining your dog at a healthy weight on nourishing food is one of the best steps you can take to ensure a lifetime of wellbeing.

Also included in this chapter are other types of problem eating. Dogs that refuse food or that are fussy eaters can be at risk of malnourishment or may be suffering from some form of underlying condition that affects their appetite. And I'll also be taking a look at the great unmentionable – dogs that eat poo.

The risks of obesity

Obesity is defined as a body weight that is 25 per cent or more above the ideal. It's as serious for dogs as it is for humans. The bottom line is that fat dogs have shorter lives. But if the health risks aren't bad enough, a dog that is obese or overweight won't enjoy what life he has to the full.

The effects of obesity:

- Increased incidence of skin disease, gastrointestinal problems and digestive disorders such as pancreatitis and diabetes.
- Organ malfunction. Too much weight puts a strain on the liver, kidneys, lungs and heart.
- Lowered immune system. Overweight dogs are more likely to succumb to various illnesses than dogs in peak condition. That means more trips to the vet.
- Poor recovery from surgery. The risk of surgery increases if a dog is overweight, because his heart and circulation are weakened.
- Loss of mobility. Fat dogs find it hard to get around. It's a vicious circle – the less they exercise, the more weight they put on. Really obese dogs may find it hard to move at all.
- Skeletal problems. Some experts believe that large- and giant-breed puppies that are allowed to grow too fast are more likely to develop congenital disorders such as hip dysplasia in later life.
- Discomfort. Fat dogs are not comfortable. Just like humans who have aches and pains, this can affect their temperament, making them more irritable and out of sorts.
- Problems in hot weather. The fatter a dog is, the harder he will find it to cope in hot weather.
- Loss of vitality. Fat dogs have no energy and they get no fun from life.

Hormones and eating habits

It is known that the female hormone oestrogen suppresses appetite. When a female first comes into heat (oestrus) she might go off her food a little and then suddenly eat more and gain weight.

When females are spayed they can also put on weight, either due to metabolic changes or because exercise has necessarily been restricted after the operation. Either way, it's a good idea to watch the food intake and resume normal levels of exercise as soon as your vet says it's OK.

Weight gain can always be controlled and should never be an excuse not to neuter a dog. As well as being the ONLY way of reducing the huge numbers of unwanted dogs that wind up in shelters every year, neutering has many positive effects on canine health. Neutered dogs of both sexes tend to live an average of two to three years longer. They are less prone to certain cancers and males are less likely to stray and get involved in accidents.

Signs of obesity

Many owners are astonished when they are told their dog is overweight. People sometimes wear blinkers where their nearest and dearest are concerned – and that includes their pets! But our perception of what a healthy dog weight looks like can also be a little skewed. With so many overweight dogs out there, a dog that is the right weight can seem positively thin by comparison. In addition, some owners may incorrectly interpret certain kinds of eating behaviour as a sign that their dog is hungry and needs more food, not less, even when the evidence of their eyes is against them.

How to tell if your dog is overweight:

- Use a touch test. While your dog is standing, run your fingers lightly down his sides over the ribs. You should be able to feel his ribs easily. A healthy dog has a thin layer of fat over the ribs, but no more. A touch test is easiest on short-haired dogs. It can be harder to feel the ribs if the coat is long and feathery.
- Use your eyes. A dog that is the right weight will have a visible waist when viewed from above. Viewed from the side, there should be a 'tuck-up' – in other words, the abdomen should slope up from the end ribcage to the thighs. Dogs that are overweight to obese have no visible waists or tuck-ups. They may also have fat along their backs and at the base of their tail.
- Weigh and compare. Consult a breed chart to find out the optimum weight range for your dog's breed. You can weigh a small dog by weighing yourself first, then picking the dog up and weighing both of you together. The dog's weight will be the difference between the two. More accurate is to take your dog to the vet and have him weighed there.
- Don't be fooled by eating behaviour. Dogs may beg for food, scavenge, and demolish everything that's put in front of them in no time flat and still be overweight. At the same time, a dog that leaves food in his bowl can also be overweight.

Medical causes of obesity

Most dogs that are obese or overweight have reached that unhappy state of affairs because they have been overfed and under-exercised. Occasionally, however, there's a medical cause for the weight gain, which is why it is important to consult your vet before you put your dog on a weight-loss programme.

The following conditions can cause weight gain or a bloated appearance. If your dog shows these symptoms, you must seek medical advice without delay:

- Under-active thyroid (hypothyroidism) shows up in weight gain, excess shedding, slow heartbeat, hair loss (especially on the tip of the tail), thin, dry skin and lethargy.
- Cushing's disease occurs when the adrenal glands become overactive and secrete an excess of steroid hormones. The stomach will bulge because the liver is enlarged. Other symptoms include increased appetite and thirst, hair loss on flanks, skin infections, lethargy, excessive panting, vomiting and muscle wastage.
- Heart or liver failure can cause fluid to build up in the abdomen, giving the stomach a distended appearance.

Consult your vet before you put your dog on a weight-loss programme.

Canine weight-watchers

Food is an important resource to a dog. It's the key to his survival. Dogs in the wild don't get fat; they're using too much energy. Food doesn't come along very often, so periods of fasting and feasting are normal. Wolves, for example, generally eat only every three to four days and then they eat as much as they possibly can. Domestic dogs are another matter entirely. Many pets are fed too much food and exercised too little. But they have no say in the matter. Being a responsible pet owner means keeping your dog in a healthy condition – if he's overweight, you need to take action.

As I mentioned at the beginning of the chapter, before you put your dog on a weight-loss programme, consult your vet. He or she will be able to recommend a practical diet plan that will result in slow and steady loss over a period of weeks and months.

There's a simple equation for weight loss: fewer calories in the diet and more exercise. If your dog is already eating nutritious high-quality food, all you need to do is reduce his intake and increase his activity levels by taking him for longer and more frequent walks.

Tips for successful dieting:

- Decrease the food gradually. Don't starve your dog or cut his rations dramatically. As with humans, slow and steady weight loss is better and puts less stress on a dog's system.
- Monitor your dog's weight at regular intervals. The recommended rate of weight loss is 8oz/250g a week for a small dog and up to 2lb/1kg a week for a large dog. Consult your vet for advice on your particular breed.
- Vegetables, cooked or raw, can help to take the edge off a dog's hunger.
- Feed your dog separately from other pets and make sure he doesn't have the chance to snack out of other food bowls. If your dog is a scavenger, keep bins locked away, and food off the kitchen counter or anywhere else he can reach.
- Only allow low-calorie treats such as strips of cooked chicken breast.
- Make sure everyone in the family understands that they are not to feed the dog more than he is allowed or to give him treats and titbits. Don't allow children to feed dogs without supervision.
- And, of course, increase the amount of exercise your dog gets (See Chapter Five, page 142).

Seasonal variations

In the summer most dogs tend to eat less, whereas they are generally hungrier in the winter when extra calories are needed to keep warm. Some northern breeds, such as huskies, are particularly predisposed to gain weight during the colder months. The extra fat gives them the energy and thermal protection they would need to pull a sled in arctic conditions. If your husky lives in the centrally heated indoors and has never seen a sled, you may need to keep an extra eye on his weight.

Food is not the same thing as love

Returning a fat dog to a healthy weight should be a relatively simple process. What complicates the matter is human motivation and emotion. People like to pamper their pets. Many owners, when they want to express affection to their dogs, pamper them with food, in the same way they would treat themselves to a nice slice of cake. When their dog gazes up at them with soulful brown eyes, they reach for the biscuit tin, or that fatty scrap left on the side of their plate. And the dog makes it crystal clear just how grateful he is!

Where food is concerned most dogs are opportunists. That's why they scavenge. An empty bowl can be enough to send some particularly food-oriented dogs off on a browsing expedition round the kitchen floor searching for any tasty morsels that might just have appeared since the last time they looked (or rather sniffed!). Very few dogs are going to turn down a treat when it's offered. The dog doesn't see you offer him a biscuit and think: 'I'm not really hungry. I just had dinner. No thanks.' He'll take his chance and that treat will be gone in a trice, even if he's already full to bursting point. And then he'll be back for more.

When you offer your dog frequent treats and snacks, especially if these are unrelated to training, you are not only devaluing a food treat as a training aid, you are teaching your dog that he'll get what he wants whenever he asks for it – cue more pleading eyes. Soon, you won't be in control of his food, he will. And if his weight shoots up as a consequence, you won't be doing him any favours as far as his long-term health is concerned.

Food is not kindness or love – it's the fuel for survival, growth and fitness. It's a hard lesson for some owners to learn. I worked with one family whose beagle, Hattie, was very overweight as a consequence of overfeeding and under-exercising. There was no structure to her diet. The food was never weighed or the portions controlled. Even the kids were contributing to Hattie's problems by offering her food round the clock. After consulting a vet, I came up with a diet plan for Hattie that should have resulted in steady weight loss – but it didn't. It wasn't Hattie's fault. The family was simply unable to resist feeding her too much. In the end Hattie was boarded out at a 'fat farm' where her intake could be monitored and she could receive the amount of exercise she needed. After a month she had lost 6½lb/3kg and was well on the road to her target weight.

For some dogs, as for some people, food becomes an antidote to boredom; it's comfort eating, if you like. If your dog doesn't have much to look forward to in his day, food will assume even greater importance to him than it would normally. What else is going to break the monotony? But there are lots of ways you can give your dog attention and stimulation without food being involved at all.

Be kind to your dogs. Show them that you care. Don't overfeed them.

Changing your dog's diet

Dogs don't just become overweight because owners feed them too much. They can also pile on the pounds if that food contains too much fat, sweeteners and starchy cereals. In other words, quality is just as important as quantity. If you feed your dog a high-quality, natural dog food it is much easier to keep him at a healthy weight.

If you decide to change your dog's diet, introduce the new food gradually. Mix a little of the new food in with what he normally gets and monitor the dog for any sign of intolerance or digestive upset. If he accepts the change, you can carry on adding more of the new food each day and decreasing the amount of the old food. The period of transition should take about a week to ten days. Taking it slowly allows the dog's digestive system to adjust to the different nutrients in his new diet.

Low-fat and prescription diets

Many pet-food companies produce special low-fat products for dogs that are overweight. Some of these contain a higher proportion of grain protein and increased amounts of fibre to bulk out the food and help satisfy the dog's hunger. There are several concerns about these products. The first is that dogs do not readily digest grain protein, which means that they may not gain the nutrients they need from these foods. The lower fat content may also show up in a poor skin and coat condition, while the increased amount of fibre will lead to bulkier, more frequent stools. The greatest risk, however, is that if a dog is kept on a low-fat diet for a considerable period of time, he may react very badly if he subsequently eats any food with a normal fat content and may even develop pancreatitis (see page 83). In general, feeding an appropriate amount of a high-quality food is a better way to reduce a dog's weight than switching to a low-fat, low-calorie product.

If your dog has a medical condition that means he must be put on a low-fat diet, however, you have no choice in the matter. Dogs who have suffered an attack of acute pancreatitis, for example, must be fed low-fat foods for the rest of their lives. Your vet will be able to recommend a suitable prescription brand.

Healthy treats

One of the reasons many dogs get fat is because their owners don't really count all those little extras they slip to their pooches all through the day – a bit of toast here, half a biscuit there, a little scrap of ham … In terms of quantity these treats may seem insignificant to us but when they're all added together they represent a huge amount of additional calories from a dog's point of view.

One study looking into the impact of nutrition in canine heart disease discovered that 90 per cent of the dogs in the survey were receiving table scraps while they were on prescription diets and medication. One of the recommendations for dogs with heart disease is to feed a low-sodium diet because salt causes water retention, which is a complication of advanced heart disease. These dogs, however, were being fed peanut butter, processed cheese and other table foods to encourage them to swallow their pills – treats that contained very high amounts of salt and which were undoing all the good of the diet and medication.

Food refusal

Appetite is a really good indicator of a dog's health. If your dog suddenly stops eating, the first thing you should do is take him to the vet. Food refusal is often the first sign of physical illness, but it can also be brought about by a number of environmental and psychological factors. Although dogs that stop eating are said to be 'anorexic' the condition is not the same as it is in humans.

If a dog won't eat for 24 hours or more, his general health will be affected regardless of what's causing the loss of appetite. Young dogs less than six months old are particularly at risk, while food refusal in puppies less than six weeks old can be life-threatening if it goes on for more than 12 hours.

Medical causes

A huge range of illnesses and conditions can cause loss of appetite and food refusal in dogs. In most cases other symptoms will also be present. These include:

- Vomiting and/or diarrhoea
- Weight loss
- Breathing difficulties
- Fever
- Excessive drooling
- Discharges (of pus or blood)
- Lethargy
- Sudden changes in behaviour.

If your dog stops eating and shows any of these symptoms, seek medical help without delay. Your vet will take a full history, examine your dog and run some tests to establish the underlying problem. Common diseases and conditions that cause loss of appetite include:

- Gastrointestinal diseases, as well as parasitic infestations, food allergies, and foreign bodies that have become stuck in the digestive tract.
- Liver diseases. The liver filters toxins from the blood. When a liver is diseased, the build-up of toxins affects the brain and dulls the appetite.
- Diseases of the pancreas.
- Kidney disease.
- Anaemia and other blood disorders.
- Dental problems. Inflamed gums can make it painful to chew.
- Ageing. As a dog ages, his sense of smell diminishes, which can make him more reluctant to eat.
- Pain of any kind.

Psychological causes

If medical causes have been ruled out, and no other symptoms are present, then the food refusal is probably due to a change in the home environment. Dogs like routine and sudden changes can make some nervous or timid individuals stressed. A new family member (human or animal), moving house, and a sudden change of diet can all trigger food refusal. So can trauma and depression.

There are a number of strategies you can try to coax your dog to eat:

- Make mealtimes sociable. Feed your dog at the same time as the rest of the family.
- Make sure his eating area is a stress-free zone, out of the main traffic routes.
- Small frequent meals may be more acceptable than two larger ones.
- Only introduce new foods very gradually. On the other hand, a new taste can sometimes tempt a dog that has gone off his regular food to eat again.
- Moisten foods and warm them slightly to just below body temperature to increase palatability. A little chopped garlic is also appetising for dogs. Never feed dogs hot food; it can scald their mouths and digestive tract. However, if your dog has come to associate a particular food with sickness or an unpleasant experience, chilling the food slightly to reduce its smell and flavour might be more successful.
- In extreme cases, you may need to hand-feed or feed with an oral syringe.

Fussy eaters

There's a fine line between fussy eating and food refusal. Sudden food refusal, especially if accompanied by other symptoms as described previously, is often the first sign of physical illness. Fussy eating, where the dog leaves some of his food, or seems to prefer certain sorts of food more than others, is often a problem that humans have created for their pets.

While it is sometimes said that toy breeds can be pickier about their food than other dogs, in my experience it is the way that owners react that is usually responsible for the behaviour. They see their dog leave some of his food and panic that he's not getting enough, so they offer a different food, usually what they regard as a 'tastier' brand. When that, too, gets left, they switch their dog's food again. Dogs do appreciate variety in their diet, but chopping and changing brands all the time can put a strain on the digestive tract.

If a dog leaves some of the food in his bowl, there's often a glaringly simple explanation: you're feeding him too much and he just isn't hungry. Not all dogs are gluttons and some will leave food uneaten when they've had enough. The answer is to reduce gradually the food you offer until the portion size is in line with your dog's appetite. At the same time, step up the exercise you give your pet and provide more stimulation through play and training.

Fussy eating is often a problem that humans have created for their pets.

Faeces eating

There's no delicate way of putting this. Some dogs eat poo – their own, or the waste of other dogs, cats or wild animals. It is actually quite normal for a dog to eat poo. However, the habit is very distressing for owners. Coprophagia, as this habit is known, is more common in young dogs, but they often grow out of it, and in dogs kept in kennels. In very rare cases coprophagia will be caused by medical problems, but other symptoms will be present too.

There are health risks associated with coprophagia – a dog may pick up a parasitic infection or harmful organisms if he eats the faeces of another animal. Provided the dog is wormed and vaccinated, he is unlikely to come to much harm if he eats his own waste.

Dietary causes

Over the years a number of theories have been put forward to explain this type of behaviour. Some people have thought that by eating faeces a dog is trying to gain some nutrients that are missing from his diet. It is certainly true that low-quality foods that contain a high proportion of grain protein can go through the gut without many nutrients being absorbed. The food comes out smelling basically the same as it went in – giving two meals for the price of one!

Another suggestion is that the taste and texture of the waste is similar to the regurgitated food a female dog will produce for her puppies. By eating faeces the dog is reminding himself of a secure time – in a sense he's comfort eating. Female dogs often eat their puppies' waste, possibly to keep the den clean so that it can't easily be tracked by predators. Puppies who witness this behaviour may copy it, with the habit continuing on into adulthood.

Behavioural causes

At least part of what causes coprophagia is probably behavioural in origin. Something about eating faeces appeals to the dog and encourages him to do it again until the habit is more engrained. He may have learned the behaviour from other dogs or he may have resorted to it because he's bored and his environment gives him no stimulation. Of course, it can also be seen as attention seeking. Nothing is more likely to provoke a reaction from an owner than the sight of their pet eating poo. It's negative attention, to be sure, but to a dog starved of company it's better than nothing.

One of the worst cases of this I ever had to deal with was a Labrador who regularly presented his returning owner with a half-eaten stool just inside the front door. That dog was also a scavenger and ate the poo of other animals as well. The owner had tried everything – putting Tabasco on the stools, feeding the dog pills that are supposed to make the faeces taste bad – and nothing had worked.

What I discovered was that the Lab had been the runt of the litter. In fact, he was the very last pup to be homed. His immediate environment gave him no stimulation and he had no toys with which to occupy himself during the periods when his owner was away from home. Quite simply, eating and playing with poo was the only way he could ease his boredom.

The first thing I did was to switch the dog to a better food that was lower in protein and contained healthy organic ingredients. Then I implemented a strict house-training/feeding schedule. Once he was fed regular meals, his elimination times could also be predicted accurately. Letting the dog out last thing at night to relieve himself reduced the risk of accidents indoors. I cleaned up the special spot where the dog liked to leave his mess using a pet deodoriser solution so no lingering smell could serve as a reminder of the habit. After that, it was a question of increasing the amount of exercise dramatically and using obedience training to stimulate him and relieve his boredom.

Obedience training can be invaluable in correcting this behaviour. The basic idea is that when the dog starts to go for the poo, you immediately interrupt his intention by making a loud noise – AH AH! – in order to stop him in his tracks. Then you distract him by directing his attention to other things.

Providing stimulating activity toys can also help to break the habit. These ease boredom in the times a dog has to be left alone and he will be less likely to feel the urge to eliminate in order to have something to play with.

There are also substances that you can get from your vet to add to your dog's food. These make the end product taste bad. Other people swear by pineapple. A little pineapple mixed into a dog's food can have the same deterrent effect.

Clean it up!

If your dog messes in the house, and especially if he is eating the poo, clean the area well to eliminate any lingering odours. You can use a special pet deodoriser, but biological washing powder will also do the trick. If he is eating faeces out of doors, restrict his opportunities to do so. For example, pick up after him immediately when he toilets in the garden.

Nothing is more likely to provoke a reaction from an owner than the sight of their pet eating poo.

Why do dogs eat grass?

The usual explanation for dogs eating grass is that they are trying to eliminate something from their system. Grass is an emetic – it induces vomiting. However, it is worth remembering that dogs as omnivores do eat vegetable matter. Some dogs will eat bark and soil, too. Others go for tissues. In some cases, this may represent an attempt to satisfy hunger with something bulky, or just to provide the pleasure of chewing. Often, it's a sign of boredom. Don't allow your dog to strip bark from trees – badly 'barked' trees will die.

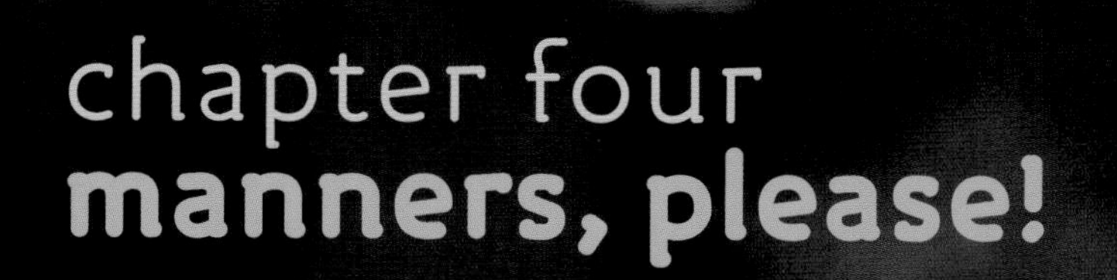

chapter four
manners, please!

So much of what we might term ‘bad behaviour’ in dogs results from our own failure to manage the home environment properly. As your dog’s leader, you have to teach him how to live in your world. He may be sharing your home with you but his instincts – particularly where food is concerned – remain pure dog.

Our homes present many tantalising temptations for dogs. When you remember how incredibly strong a dog’s sense of smell is, it’s no wonder some of our smarter four-legged friends devote a lot of brainpower to working out how to get into the dustbin. I know dogs that can open fridges.

Behavioural issues related to food come in a variety of forms. One type, which includes scavenging, stealing and food guarding, can be addressed by positive training and preventative measures. Another, which shows up in problems with temperament, such as aggression and hyperactivity, may have its roots in poor nutrition. Diet can have a big impact on a dog’s mood. Other troublesome issues include digging, excessive licking and flatulence, which I’ll be covering later in the chapter.

Begging

Dogs that constantly beg for food have often learned this behaviour from their owners. If you feed your dog scraps from your plate or let him share your biscuit, you've only got yourself to blame when you find him glued to your side, whimpering and drooling, every time you have something to eat. After all, he knows which side his bread is buttered on!

Another type of begging takes the form of the dog 'nagging' you to fill up his food bowl. He may do this in various ways – by barking and whining, by dancing around you every time you come into the kitchen or approach the fridge, or by sitting with his expectant, pleading eyes trained on you. Nine times out of ten what causes this behaviour is boredom. Mealtimes are high points in a dog's day. If nothing much else is happening, he'll see if he can't persuade you to feed him a couple more times just to liven things up a bit. Given the choice between a walk and more food, a dog that has been doing his utmost to tell you he is starving will forget all about his stomach when he sees you reach for the lead.

Here are some rules to deal with begging:

- Make a clear distinction between your food and your dog's food. Don't feed your dog from your plate. If he hovers when you're cooking, ask him to stay in his basket or shut him out of the kitchen. See also the technique for keeping a dog in his basket on page 123.
- Give your dog treats as rewards for good behaviour or during training, not randomly or because he asks.
- Stick to set feeding times. If you are feeding your dog a high-quality food and he's showing no signs of dietary intolerance, he's not hungry, he's bored.
- Remember that food is no substitute for stimulation, company and fun.
- Make your dog work for his food. Tell him to SIT until the bowl is on the floor, then give the release command OK.

Sit!

Cue or signal: Hold your hand in front of your dog's nose, then raise your wrist slightly.

'Sit!' is one of the simplest commands to teach. Sitting is a natural posture for dogs. Start early and train your puppy to sit and wait for his food.

Here's how it works:

- Equip yourself with a treat. Hold it between your thumb, index and third finger with your palm facing upwards.
- Call your dog. Puppies learn their names really quickly and he should come over to investigate.
- Show the dog you have a treat in your hand. Hold it in front of his nose. Let him sniff it, lick it, paw it, but don't let him have it.
- At this stage, don't utter a command or say anything at all.
- Eventually, your dog will sit. Now here is where you need split-second timing. You have to catch that action and reward it on the spot. Don't say anything, just give him the treat.
- Repeat the same procedure two more times. Wait for the action, catch it, give him the treat and praise him.
- The next step is to put in the vocal cue and signal. As your dog is in the act of sitting, say SIT and raise your wrist slightly. Repeat this five to ten times.
- Finally, ask your dog to SIT, using the hand signal, before he has started to sit. Repeat the same sequence five to ten times.
- If he doesn't SIT when you ask him to, don't repeat the command. Take the treat immediately out of reach, removing it up to shoulder level, and say 'UH OH!' Wait a couple of seconds and try again.
- Always give lots of praise after a session.

Stealing and scavenging

I've known some smart dogs in my time but one of the cleverest dogs I've ever met was a female Dalmatian called Dally. Dally could open the front door and the back door. In fact, she could open any door in the house – including the doors of the kitchen cupboards, top and bottom, the door of the microwave and the oven door. She could also turn the microwave and oven on.

All that intelligence was directed at one thing – food. Dally was so obsessed with food that she could not settle down if food was anywhere in the vicinity. When her owner started to cook, Dally would pace, salivate and generally make a nuisance. She was literally beside herself.

When a dog gets under your feet when you're cooking, the simplest (and safest) course of action is to keep him out of the kitchen. Most people don't mind a little sniffing around their ankles when they're preparing dinner and some owners become very adept at the kind of fancy footwork that stops them from tripping over a dog that has positioned himself right under the counter in hopes that a scrap might fall his way. But handling sharp implements and carrying hot dishes and pans from oven to counter or table are hazardous enough without having to run an obstacle course. Unfortunately, in Dally's case shutting her out of the kitchen wasn't practical. First, there were her door-opening skills to reckon with. Secondly, the way the house was arranged meant that there was nowhere else for her basket to be. What I did was to train her to stay in her basket when food was around. The key to that was making her basket a place where good things happened.

Here's how the method works:

- Make sure there is no food left out in the kitchen.
- Tell your dog to go to his bed and STAY.
- After a minute or so, go back to the basket and give a treat.
- Then give the release command OK.
- Repeat the exercise, gradually extending the intervals so that the dog is staying for longer periods between treats.
- Then introduce some food into the kitchen and put it on the counter. When I tried this exercise with Dally, I started with crisps because they aren't too strong-smelling.
- Repeat the exercise, extending the intervals and bringing out more food, working up to the greatest temptation, meat.
- Once your dog can stay in the basket for half an hour while food is being cooked you can stop treating him each time he obeys and offer rewards intermittently.

This type of training represents only half the solution. While I was training Dally to remain calm in the presence of food I also worked on redirecting her excessive focus on food back to her owner, using obedience training, games and play. And, most importantly, all of Dally's food came through her owner. Many dogs that are food-obsessed are bored. More opportunities for exercise and mental stimulation – and more company – usually turn this type of situation around.

Other measures may also be required. Another dog I've worked with called Buster had some rather shocking habits. He would jump up on the kitchen counter and pee on the bread bin, microwave and knife-block. He was also a pretty good thief and had been known to open the oven and steal the Sunday roast. What I did on this occasion was to send out the message that the kitchen counter was an unpleasant place to be. We set up a system so that every time Buster headed for the counter an alarm went off. This avoidance technique helped to break the association between the kitchen counter and food in Buster's mind.

Who ate the cheese?

Most dogs don't have the kind of superior mental skills that allowed Dally to work out how to open a kitchen wall cupboard and snack on the contents. The following basic rules are usually enough to cut opportunities for scavenging and food theft down to a bare minimum:

- Put food away. Large dogs are perfectly capable of jumping up on kitchen counters to get what their noses tell them is up there. Even a smaller dog will hop from chair to tabletop to polish off your half-eaten pasta while you answer the doorbell. Get into the habit of removing food dishes from the table every time you leave the room or get up from your chair (many dogs move like greased lightning when food's left lying around).
- Don't leave rubbish bags unattended. Dogs who smell the delicious treats inside (garbage to you, gourmet nosh to them) will rip through polythene and devour the contents, which may include all kinds of positively harmful things – poultry bones, fatty scraps and other foods that can cause digestive upsets and worse. Lock your bin in a cupboard or buy a bin that has a catch fastening. Robust bins are also more secure as they can't be toppled easily.
- Don't attempt to correct a dog for scavenging or stealing unless you catch him at it. You can only correct a dog within *one second* of the undesired behaviour. Otherwise, he won't have a clue what he's being told off about.
- Take special precautions when children are around. Children sometimes tease dogs with food. In any case, small children are much nearer the dog's feeding level – the floor – than adults and the food they hold in their hands can present an overwhelming temptation to a dog. Make sure children eat at the table when the dog is around or remove the dog from the picture.
- Take special care at holiday times. Vets report a much higher incidence of serious digestive upsets, including pancreatitis, around holiday times – Christmas, New Year, Thanksgiving. One reason is that owners decide to 'treat' their dogs to some of the same goodies they're eating themselves, which are often the highly fatty foods that can be so harmful to dogs. Another cause is the influx of guests and family members who may not be aware that sugary and fatty treats play havoc with a dog's digestion and can even be life-threatening. And, of course, holidays and social get-togethers are generally occasions when people let their hair down and naturally become less vigilant as a consequence. Uncle Harry's telling one of his funny stories and no one notices the dog scoffing the cake ... The safest course of action is to keep pets shut in a quiet room during parties.

Leave it!

No hand signal.

Stealing becomes much more serious, at least as far as we humans are concerned, when a dog tries to snatch food out of your hand. One of the dogs I've worked with on my programme, a Labrador/whippet cross called Lucy, would literally attempt to snatch a sandwich as it was going into her owner's mouth. You don't need me to tell you that this kind of behaviour can result in a bad bite. One way of dealing with snatching is to teach your dog the LEAVE IT command. This is a useful, all-purpose command that has other applications outside food.

Here's how it works:

- Close your hand around a treat, leaving a little sticking out so that the dog does not have easy access to it. Let him sniff it.
- As soon as he pulls his head away from the treat, praise him and give him the treat.
- Repeat these steps a couple of times, then add the command LEAVE IT.
- As soon as he hesitates or looks away from the treat, praise him and give him the treat.
- The next stage is to use two treats. Place a treat in your open hand and repeat the steps, except this time, you reward the dog with the treat you have in your other (closed) hand.
- Follow this up by putting a treat on the floor. Repeat the process, rewarding your dog with the treat you have in your hand, not the one on the floor.
- Finally, put your dog on a lead and walk him past the treat on the floor. As he goes to get the treat, say LEAVE IT. The moment he stops or looks at you, give lots of praise and reward with the treat that you have in your hand and not the one on the floor.
- Keep repeating the exercise with the dog on the lead. Place other objects on the floor, preferably the type of things you want him to leave alone. It may be the bin, for example. Once your dog is doing well with this command in the house, you can start to use it outside.

Drop it!

No hand signal.

The worst has happened and your dog has something in his mouth you don't want him to have. It may be a lethal chicken bone, it may be your designer shoe, it may be a child's toy. Whatever it is, you want it out of his mouth now.

Most of the time when a dog has something in his mouth, you have to accept that it now belongs to the dog, particularly when that something is food. Even a pack leader will not challenge a dog of lower status over a piece of meat. How would we feel if someone reached into our mouths and grabbed food out of it? If your dog has got hold of a piece of bread, it's best to let him eat it. If it's a chicken bone, however, you can't afford to take the risk.

Try to get the bone out of the dog's mouth by prising open his jaws. Dogs have very strong jaws and you will need to be very careful not to get yourself bitten in the process. If you have a delicious treat on hand – some cooked chicken or liver – you may be able to get your dog to relinquish the bone himself. But it has to be a higher trade.

You stand a better chance of success of getting a dog to drop something from his mouth if you have trained him from an early age that dropping objects can be fun and the source of pleasure. One solution is the 'take it and drop it' game.

Here's how it works:

- Equip yourself with five or so different toys that your dog likes. Try to choose his favourites. Each toy should be slightly higher in value than the one before, that is, it should be more interesting to the dog.
- The first step is to teach your dog the command TAKE IT. Out of those five objects, choose the toy that has the lowest value as far as your dog is concerned. Call your dog and show him the object. As he begins to open his mouth to take it, say TAKE IT. Then when he has taken the toy, praise him.
- Let him have some time with the toy, running and playing.
- Now you get another toy of slightly more interest to the dog and put it in your other hand. Call your dog and show him the object. A dog will naturally relinquish something that he perceives as plain OK for something he sees as better. As soon as he drops the first object, say DROP IT. Then praise him. Immediately give him the other object and say TAKE IT. Praise him when he does.
- Then leave him to play a while with the second object.
- Repeat the 'take it and drop it' game until you reach the last object. Make sure it's a real bonus for the dog. A chew, perhaps.
- Allow him to chew on it for a while, then produce another chew. Say DROP IT to ask him to drop the chew he has in his mouth, and say TAKE IT as you offer him the second one. This teaches him to give up high-value, tasty things as well.

Food guarding

Dogs are naturally protective of a resource as important to them as food. Some dogs, perhaps because of past experiences, take this protectiveness a stage further and growl or lash out if anyone approaches their bowl. Rescue dogs, for example, may have had to fight for their food, which can make the whole business of eating an anxious time for them. The answer isn't to stay well clear, but to train your dog that your presence near his bowl means that good things happen to him. (Please note that small children should not be allowed to do this kind of training.)

The technique is a version of the method I use to teach puppies that I am their food source and not a threat (see page 70).

Here's how it works:

- Prepare the dog's food in the usual way.
- Then set down an empty bowl. The dog will go for the bowl, see there is nothing in it and look at you.
- As he looks at you, praise him and throw a little food into the empty bowl from a distance. He will eat it. Then throw in a little bit more. Repeat this until he has finished his meal.
- Make no attempt to pick up the bowl before he has finished.
- For the next month, carry on throwing food into the empty bowl at every single meal. For the first week, keep on doing this from a distance. Then gradually move closer until you are able to stand right by him. Always praise him when he looks up at you, then add food to his bowl.
- Never push a dog too fast. If he begins to guard at any stage, move back a level in your training.
- Try approaching his bowl from different directions, always keeping food in your hand. Varying the picture in this way will help your dog feel relaxed if his bowl is approached from different angles and by different people.
- The last stage is to touch your dog as you throw food into the bowl. First, you touch him for a second, gradually working up to a small stroke. You might even try touching his bowl. Be careful with this. Only touch his bowl as if by accident when you are putting the food in.

Fighting over food

Food guarding can escalate into all-out warfare if you have two or more dogs in your home, especially if those dogs tend to fight over other resources such as toys. Often this is a question of an older, larger or more dominant animal trying to show the other one who's boss. Training does not have a role in this type of situation, but management does. Separate the dogs and feed them, at the same time, in different rooms, behind closed doors. Allow them each 20 minutes to finish the food, then remove the bowls and let them be together again.

Diet and mood

I've worked with dogs that display all kinds of behavioural problems. In every case, the first question I ask the owners is 'What do you give your dog to eat?' Poor nutrition has many negative outcomes, including obesity and disease. It can also show up in aggression, hyperactivity, compulsions and other anxiety disorders.

Serious behavioural problems – such as canine aggression – can be very complex to understand and treat. Many factors may be involved, including underlying physical disorders, a traumatic event in the dog's past, side effects of medication, and poor socialisation and handling. But diet also has a role to play. Changing a dog that has been fed a cheap commercial product to a more nutritious food can make a big difference in his temperament. Studies have shown that high-protein diets can predispose a dog to aggression and hyperactivity. So can many of the chemical additives and preservatives found in cheaper foods.

Happy chemicals

Like humans, dogs need adequate levels of a chemical called serotonin in their brains in order to feel calm and to regulate their sleeping and waking patterns. Too little serotonin causes anxiety, aggression and hyperactivity, common behavioural problems in dogs.

Serotonin is synthesised in the brain from an amino acid called tryptophan, which is the least abundant of all the amino acids that a dog needs for health, wellbeing and growth. Like other amino acids, tryptophan is found in protein foods. It is plentiful in turkey meat and is also found in oats, cottage cheese, bananas, meat, fish and chicken.

It has been discovered that carbohydrates also play an important role in the synthesis of serotonin by serving to increase the concentration of tryptophan in the bloodstream. Some dogs that suffer from stress disorders such as aggression can benefit from tryptophan supplements or a diet that combines an easily digestible protein with carbohydrate. They should never be fed products that contain corn, which lowers tryptophan levels.

Prolonged periods of exercise – for example, a good workout rather than a few short walks – similarly raise tryptophan levels. At the same time, exercise releases endorphins, other 'happy chemicals' responsible for feelings of pleasure throughout the body.

It's only natural

Dogs exhibit a number of other food-related behaviours that may seem strange to us. To dogs, they're only natural.

Digging

Some dogs love to dig and may bury their bones in the garden – often under your favourite shrub! For certain breeds, digging is a food-related behaviour in the sense that it's a way of tracking burrowing prey such as badgers, moles and rabbits. It has also been suggested that wild dogs may bury bones as a means of tenderising them through decay. If your dog's digging behaviour is wreaking havoc on your garden, or he's burying his bones in the sofa, one solution is to provide him with a sandpit where he can hide his bones and toys to his heart's content. You can't stop him digging, but you can redirect the behaviour so he still has his fun and your plants are undisturbed.

One of the dogs that I've worked with displayed some very unusual digging behaviour. Lotty was a Patterdale terrier/Labrador mix. Ever since the owners' garden had been laid to turf, Lotty had been digging frenziedly everywhere. The odd thing about it was that she hadn't dug in the garden at all when the ground was bare soil. She had other compulsions, too. She licked fences, brickwork, walls and the ground. She chased her tail and she chased reflections everywhere. That dog was in perpetual motion.

What I discovered was that Lotty was a rescue dog who had suffered a terrible upbringing. For three months her previous owners had kept her in a shed with nothing to play with and no company. Terriers are hard-wired to chase moving prey and it seemed to me that what Lotty had learned to do was to chase light – it was the only thing that had moved in the dismal surroundings she had been raised in. Unlike bare soil, grass is very reflective, each blade glinting in the sun. Lotty was chasing the light across the grass and digging where it was reflected, just as a terrier will chase prey and dig where the rat or mole goes to earth.

What I did was redirect Lotty's digging to a more suitable location. We gave her a sandpit where she could play with her toys and I set up a pole with a crystal on top, directed to reflect shining patches of light onto the sandpit.

Licking

Licking is an important oral behaviour for a dog. When a pup is born, his mother will lick him all over to clean him and stimulate his respiratory system. She will also lick the anal and genital area to encourage elimination. Wild pups lick around their mother's mouth to stimulate her to regurgitate half-digested food, a gesture that survives into adulthood as a sign of submission. When your dog licks your face, it's not a kiss. He's not saying 'I love you', he's saying 'I'm no threat' or 'Please feed me'.

Licking is also soothing for a dog. It releases those pleasure chemicals in the brain. Just like thumb-sucking in humans, dogs sometimes use licking as a way of comforting themselves when they are anxious. Long after the environmental stress has gone the habit lingers on. Compulsive licking, particularly of paws, wrists and hocks, can become almost addictive and dogs may carry on licking even after the area becomes inflamed. A dog may also repeatedly lick a certain spot if that area is painful, or if sensation is dulled there due to compromised nerve endings. Labs and other retrievers, Dobermans and Great Danes tend to show this type of behaviour more than other breeds. Dobermans that are bored or have suffered maternal deprivation also tend to suck blankets and cushions.

Relieving any stress that might be bothering the dog is one answer, and of course you must also rule out any condition such as arthritis that might be causing a dog pain. Redirecting the behaviour by increasing opportunities for fun and games can help to break the habit. It's no good telling a dog off when he licks. Distract him by offering him a more positive experience but be careful that he doesn't see licking as a way of getting your attention.

I once worked with a boxer that used licking to demonstrate the various ways he was unhappy. He was kept in a fenced yard for prolonged periods of time while his owners were at work and would lick the fence and try to jump over it every time he heard the next-door neighbours come out into their garden. He licked everyone who came to the door and particularly liked to lick the male of the house. He'd lick him on the top of his bald head after he'd been jogging.

The fence-licking was the way the dog communicated that he was bored and needed company. Licking people on the doorstep was a gesture of passivity that was also a little bit controlling. It showed that the dog was not comfortable with strangers and became a coping mechanism. Licking the man of the house was also a passive gesture – although what the dog was after when he licked his owner's head after he'd been jogging was salt.

That dog needed a much more stimulating day. I also worked with the owners to show them how to distract the dog from his licking behaviour and direct his attention to more positive things.

Chasing

Dogs see moving objects much better than they do stationary ones. In the wild, this gives them a natural advantage when it comes to hunting down prey. A dog that chases anything that moves – squirrel, cat, bird – is responding to an instinctive prey-driven trigger. But while he may enjoy the thrill of the chase he is much less likely to harm next door's cat in the unlikely event that he corners her. Chasing can be a problem, however, when it puts the dog in danger. Chasing cars is an obvious example. Keep your dog on a lead in busy areas at all times and make sure he doesn't have the opportunity to dash out of the house into the path of oncoming traffic in hot pursuit of a cat or squirrel. Keep garden areas adequately fenced for the same reason. Chasing and retrieving games in the park are a good way of redirecting this behaviour.

Tugging and shaking

Many terriers worry away at their toys and bones. Dogs bred to kill rats dispatch their prey by a violent shaking that breaks the rodent's neck. These breeds often enjoy games of tug of war.

Flatulence

Flatulence is one of those issues that arouse either hilarity or acute social embarrassment. If your dog breaks wind frequently, you might find yourself rushing around with the air freshener, opening windows and apologising profusely to your guests. At the very least, you'll probably move further down the sofa. But flatulence in a dog sometimes needs to be investigated. It can be a sign of an allergy, dietary intolerance or another medical problem.

Recently when I was filming Ramah, an Egyptian Pharaoh hound, she passed such terrible wind that the cameraman had to stick his head out of the window for a while, and this is a guy who has had a lot of experience around dogs and knows what kind of unsavoury things they can get up to. Ramah's diet contained milk and eggs, which was a contributing factor to the sulphurous smell.

Most of the wind dogs pass is odourless and is the result of swallowing air. Dogs that bolt their food are taking in a lot of air. Keeping mealtimes stress-free and eating zones calm and out of the way of traffic can help. Exercise also helps the dog's digestive system to function properly and prevents an excess build-up of gas.

Other causes of flatulence include:

- Too much fibre in the diet.
- Poorly digestible food, such as the fillers found in cheap dog food.
- Dietary intolerance. This may be caused by a certain kind of grain or protein in the diet or simply reflect the fact that the dog has scavenged something that's upset his system. Many dogs are lactose-intolerant and should not be given milk.
- Diseases of the pancreas or intestinal tract. Other symptoms such as vomiting, diarrhoea, poor appetite and weight loss will generally also be present.

Anal glands

While we're on unpleasant subjects, another problem that can be food-related is blockage of the dog's anal glands. These are located either side of the anus and discharge a strong scent that serves as a territorial marker. They also collect waste matter. Feeding a dog a poor diet can cause these glands to become blocked. The dog will display his discomfort by dragging his rear on the ground. If you notice your dog rubbing his rear on the ground, or starting to nibble parts of his body or feet, this might be a sign of referred discomfort from compacted anal glands and you should take him to the vet. Treatment involves expressing the contents of the glands manually. Increasing the amount of fibre in the diet is also sometimes recommended, although some experts believe this can cause other dietary problems.

chapter five

walkies!

As the saying goes, if your dog is overweight, you're not getting enough exercise. Like us, dogs need exercise to keep fit and maintain a healthy weight. But as well as toning muscles and reducing fat, a good workout releases happy chemicals in the brain. It's a powerful de-stressor for dogs and humans alike.

A fat dog is obviously overfed and under-exercised. But even dogs that are at an appropriate weight suffer when their owners give them short shrift as far as exercise is concerned. Dogs that are not provided with the mental and physical stimulation that exercise delivers often develop behavioural problems and compulsions because they are depressed, frustrated and bored.

Dogs and humans have lived happily side by side for thousands of years. That doesn't mean that our homes are natural environments for dogs. The kind of sensory stimulation that a dog particularly enjoys can't be found in the average living room – it's out there in the open air.

Why are so many dogs short-changed when it comes to exercise? I think there are several explanations. First, to put it bluntly, some owners are just plain lazy. Or they see dog walking as a chore to be done with as quickly as possible. Others may have encountered problems that have put them off exercising their dogs as often as they should. Maybe the dog pulls on the lead, runs off, gets into fights with other dogs, or behaves badly around people when he's let off the lead. The answer is not to go for shorter, fewer walks, but to train the dog properly.

The benefits of exercise

Exercise is key to every dog's wellbeing. Here's why:

- It maintains muscle tone and mass.
- It promotes healthy skeletal development.
- It raises the metabolic rate so that toxins are flushed out of the system more efficiently.
- It helps the digestive system to work effectively.
- It helps keep weight levels down and reduces fat.
- It stimulates the production of serotonin and endorphins in the brain, chemicals that give pleasure, promote calmness and reduce stress levels.
- It provides the dog with sensory stimulation by exposing him to different environments.
- It satisfies a dog's inherent need to work.
- It provides opportunities for dogs to socialise with other dogs and humans. Dogs are not solitary creatures – they need company.

Like the right diet, the right level of exercise delivers benefits all round. A well-exercised dog will live longer and that life will be happier, too.

A natural high

Studies have shown that prolonged exercise, such as endurance trials, releases more of the happy chemicals and relieves stress better than short, frequent periods of exercise.

Have dog, will travel

Taking your dog out for regular walks and runs off the lead is a great way of reinforcing the bond between you. If you train your dog properly, a whole world of great excursions will open up for both him and you – runs on the beach, walks through the woods, country rambles ... Then it won't just be your dog who looks forward to 'Walkies!'

Vary the picture

When it comes to exercise, quality is just as important as quantity. Taking the same route to the same park twice a day and letting your dog off the lead to run free in the same fenced area is just as boring for the dog as it is for you. He needs new things to explore. Try a different route or a different park. Get in the car and drive to a different area altogether. Variety is the spice of life.

It's a myth that dogs will exercise themselves if you leave them in the back garden all day. What is likely to get the most exercise is their vocal cords as they relieve their frustration and loneliness through barking. Dogs will run up and down fence lines if someone passes by – or another animal comes into view – but a dog left alone in a back garden for long periods is not appreciably happier than one left alone in the house.

Your dog needs new things to explore.

Safe walking

Dog walking isn't high up there on the list of extreme sports but there are some common-sense guidelines to bear in mind to ensure you and your dog walk safely.

- Choose the appropriate collar and lead for your dog's size and make sure they fit properly (see page 152).
- Make sure your dog's identification and licence tags are fixed to his collar. You should also have your dog micro-chipped, a cheap, painless procedure in which a small disc is inserted under the skin, giving the dog his own unique bar code.
- Equip yourself with a bottle of water and a collapsible nylon water bowl so that you can give your dog a drink if he needs one.
- Take a supply of plastic bags so you can clean up after your dog.
- Wear reflective gear when walking a dog after dark or in a poorly lit area. Put reflective tags on your dog's collar and lead.
- Always keep your dog on a lead when you are walking him along a street or a road. This is a legal requirement in some areas. Only let him off the lead in a park or any other open space where it is safe for him to run. Respect the 'dog-free' areas in parks and public spaces. Many beaches are closed to dogs in high season.
- Before you start letting your dog off the lead, make sure he is responding well to the COME command (see page 172). This has to be really solid before you can expect him to come back to you reliably. Use your common sense. Even the best-trained animal is going to find it hard to resist some things. If you can spot an obvious temptation on the horizon, keep your dog on the lead for the time being.
- Be careful around water, especially in bad weather. Every year there are tragic accidents where owners drown trying to save pets that have fallen into rivers or been swept out to sea.
- Don't let your dog drink from puddles in the street as they could contain antifreeze. Antifreeze, which has a sweet taste that appeals to dogs, is lethal. Even a small amount can kill.
- Avoid areas that have been recently sprayed with insecticides or chemicals.
- Wipe your dog's feet after walking him in cold weather to get rid of road salt that he might otherwise lick off and ingest.
- In summer try to avoid going out at the hottest times of the day. Walk your dog in the early morning or early evening when it's cooler.

Choosing leads and collars

There is a huge range of dog-walking equipment on the market. Many leads and collars are expressly designed to correct common problems, such as pulling on the lead. With a few exceptions, I don't believe in such quick-fix approaches. The way to get your dog to walk properly on the lead is to teach him, not to hurt him, which is what some of these devices do. Here are some factors to consider:

- Material. Dog leads and collars come in nylon, cotton, leather and chain metal. My preference is for nylon or cotton. Both are comfortable, durable, washable and do not become brittle when wet as leather does. Chain leads can slip through the hands.
- Size. Wider leads and collars are suitable for larger dogs. A retriever, for example, needs a collar that is about 1 inch/2.5cm in width. Greyhounds, whippets and borzois, who have heads that are about the same size or smaller than their necks, need even wider collars. As far as lead length is concerned, I generally find that a 6 foot/1.8 metre lead is about right for walking a dog in a public place. If the lead is too short, it will be tight and tense and the dog is more likely to resist it; if it's too long, you won't have control.
- Extendable leads. These leads come in a variety of lengths, with 12 feet/3.6 metres and 30 feet/9 metres being the most common. An extendable lead is useful for giving a dog a little more freedom but should only be used in a park or open space because it doesn't give you the same degree of control as a standard lead does. Choose the right lead for your dog's weight, according to the recommendations printed on the packaging. Shorter extendables can snap if used on a heavier dog. I do use extendables in my work but I wouldn't recommend the alternative, which is the stretch lead, because it can sometimes stretch further than it is supposed to.
- Harnesses. These fit round the body and distribute pressure evenly, which makes them good for small dogs with delicate necks.
- Martingales. This type of collar has a double-loop design that tightens and loosens according to how tense the lead is. It's a good choice for whippets, greyhounds and borzois.

Please don't choke me!

Stay well clear of choke chains, choke collars and prong or pinch collars. They hurt dogs, sometimes seriously. If used incorrectly or inexpertly, dogs can suffer collapsed windpipes; there have also been a number of deaths from misuse. Similarly slip leads can also choke dogs. I only ever use a slip lead when I'm working with an aggressive or sensitive dog that doesn't like to be handled around the head.

Levels of activity

Dogs vary in the amounts of exercise they need, which is why it is difficult to give hard and fast rules about how much exercise is enough. One important variable is age. Puppies and young dogs are still growing and too much exercise can put a strain on their bodies. Older dogs are slowing down and require different exercise regimes than healthy adults in the peak of fitness. Then there are certain breed differences to take into account, as well as possible health issues. Before you make any major changes to the way you exercise your dog, it is always a good

Exercising puppies

Left to their own devices, puppies will naturally exercise as much as they need to and no more. That exercise will generally come in the form of play – romping with littermates and exploring their surroundings. The rest of the time will be spent sleeping. Short bursts of playful activity will alternate with naps throughout the day.

Puppies have loose joints and ligaments and their bones are not fully developed until approximately 18 months, with the larger and giant breeds taking longer to reach physical maturity. For this reason, it is very important that puppies and young dogs should not be over-exercised. Too much exercise as well as exercise of the wrong kind can damage joints and muscles and cause problems in later life. Avoid agility training or endurance trials until your dog is 18 months old.

Tips for exercising puppies:

- Playing allows puppies to exercise their muscles all round without undue stress. Use toys and games to have fun together. Keep sessions short so your puppy does not get too tired.
- Let your puppy explore your garden, but make sure it is safely fenced. Puppies need to go outside straight after eating to encourage them to eliminate.
- Basic obedience training can begin as soon as you get your puppy home. Teach him basic commands and get him used to wearing a collar and lead (see page 165).
- After 16 weeks of age puppies start to greet new experiences much more cautiously so it is a good idea to start taking him out before he reaches this stage to get him used to the smells, sights and sounds of the outside world. Keep walks short – 20 minutes to half an hour a day – to begin with. The idea is not to provide exercise as such, it's to expose the puppy to as many new things as possible so he socialises well around other dogs and humans and gets used to his new environment.
- Build up exercise very gradually. By the time your dog is six months old, two half-hour sessions is about right.
- Monitor how much running your puppy does. Puppies don't have the stamina of older dogs and can tire easily.
- Offer plenty of water. Puppies also overheat more quickly than adult dogs. Don't allow a puppy (or an adult dog) to drink a massive amount of water in one go. Frequent small drinks are better.
- Don't allow your puppy to jump or to engage in any other physical activity that might damage his joints until he is fully developed. The hips are particularly vulnerable.

Exercising adult dogs

All healthy adult dogs need a combination of regular walking and free running off the lead. A glorious run every day is every dog's birthright and it's the biggest stress-buster around. Freedom also allows a dog to set his own pace, which is often slower than you might expect – after all, it takes time and concentration to give all those new smells the attention they deserve! Take the time to train your dog so that he's safe and sociable off the lead and can enjoy what nature intended him for.

Walking on a lead is an unnatural activity for a dog. But it's a skill he has to learn (see page 166). All dogs should be kept on leads in urban areas where they could otherwise cause accidents. I often use an extendable lead when I'm exercising dogs in open spaces near main roads. These can be a good halfway measure if for some reason you simply cannot let your dog off the lead at all.

My grandmother, who bred beagles, was a huge inspiration to me in my work. Five times a week she used to walk her dogs down to some big fields near her home and let them run to their hearts' content. Twice a week, she did what she called 'roadwork' with them. This involved walking the dogs on the pavement. The pads of domestic dogs aren't as durable as those of wild dogs and can be overly sensitive without regular exposure to hard surfaces. Walking on concrete helps to strengthen the pads and keeps the nails trim. My grandmother hardly ever had to clip her dogs' nails.

My preference is to give dogs three exercise sessions a day, two long periods morning and afternoon and a shorter walk later on. Staggering the exercise periods breaks up the day and gives dogs something to look forward to. I always exercise the dogs an hour after or an hour before feeding. Dogs, like humans, aren't comfortable being exercised on full stomachs and it can cause problems such as bloating.

If you're going to be out for a while or you are exercising your dog particularly strenuously or exercising in hot weather, be sure to take a water bottle with you. Give him water at regular intervals, but don't allow him to drink too much at one time.

Exercising older dogs

An ageing dog still needs exercise. But little and often is generally better than extended workouts. While many dogs enjoy exercise well into their later years most begin to slow down a little. Some dogs go deaf and/or blind in old age; others develop conditions such as arthritis that can make movement difficult. As your dog ages, you will have to modify the type of activity he engages in and reduce the amount of exercise to a level that he's comfortable with.

Nothing upsets me more than seeing some poor old dog being dragged through the park, huffing and puffing. As your dog ages, you will have to accept that he won't be able to do as much as he used to. Talk to your vet and make common-sense adjustments to your dog's exercise regime.

NOTE: If your older dog becomes breathless easily or coughs, this can be a sign of heart disease. Take him to your vet.

Breed variations

Different breeds vary in their need for physical exercise. Dogs that have been bred to track, hunt, retrieve or herd generally require much more exercise, particularly free running, than toy or companion animals such as cavalier King Charles spaniels or bichon frises, that are just as happy on a lap or snuggled in a tote bag as they are in the park. Size is not an infallible guide, however. Jack Russell terriers are small dogs but they have terrific energy and need proper workouts.

Dogs with flattened faces, such as bulldogs and pugs, must be exercised with care. Because these dogs have restricted breathing, they have a tendency to overheat easily, which means you should avoid prolonged or rigorous exercise sessions.

Exercising overweight dogs

Exercise and diet are the two sides of the fitness equation. If your dog needs to lose weight, you will have to decrease the amount you are feeding him and increase the amount of exercise.

It's very important to increase the amount of exercise gradually. Fat or overweight dogs that have led a fairly sedentary life are at risk of injury or strain if they are suddenly subjected to prolonged workouts. It's a psychological shock to their systems as much as a physical one. Start gently with 20-minute sessions three times a day. As your dog begins to lose weight, his energy levels will rise and you can increase the amount of exercise accordingly. See page 183 for special exercise regimes using treadmills and hydrotherapy.

Lead work

The key to really enjoyable walks with your dog lies in basic training. Teach him to walk well on the lead and you'll be able to take him just about anywhere!

How to introduce your puppy to a collar and lead

Collars and leads are new to most puppies, as they generally have never experienced such restraints before leaving the litter. The throat is a very vulnerable area on the dog's body and his instinct is to protect it. Many dogs also do not like the feeling of something going over their head and invading their personal space.

Introduce your puppy to the collar first. Put it on for a few seconds. Try not to put it on over his head, but unbuckle it and do it up from the underside of the puppy's neck. Don't do it up too tightly; just let it sit lightly around his throat. Give him praise and rewards. Then take it off. Gradually build up the period of time you leave the collar on the puppy, using positive feedback, until he gets used to the sensation. Each time tighten the collar a little more until it cannot slip over his head. Some dogs take longer to get used to collars than others. Once your dog is used to the collar, leave it on.

The next step is to introduce the lead. Clip it on to the puppy's collar and call his name. Praise and treat him when he comes to you. Practise putting the lead on and taking it off, rewarding calm behaviour. This gets the puppy used to the idea of the lead. Always accustom a puppy to the collar and lead before you take him out of doors, when he will have all kinds of other new sensations to deal with.

Some dogs take longer to get used to collars than others.

How to teach your dog to walk on a lead

Start training your puppy how to walk with you as soon as he is accustomed to his collar and lead. Practise around the house and out in the garden first before taking him out in the street or to the park where there will be more distractions.

Teaching your dog to walk properly on a lead is a really key part of dog training. If you do not teach him how to do it, he will pull and your daily walks with him will turn into constant struggles for control. But if a dog shouldn't pull, you shouldn't either. NEVER yank a puppy along on his lead. You could do serious damage to his throat.

It's really important to begin this type of training as early as possible. For a start, it's easier to teach a puppy how to walk in the right way on the lead than it is to correct an older dog once he has been dragging you around for months. Secondly, puppies grow. If you own one of the larger breeds, by the time your dog's bad walking habits are well and truly established, he may be big enough to pull you over or drag you into traffic.

Walking well on a lead is different to heeling. Before teaching your dog to heel, first you have to teach your dog to walk without pulling, to walk where you walk and not in a direction of his own choosing, and to stop when you stop.

The lead transmits your feelings direct to the dog. If you are tense, the dog will feel it. Many people seize a lead and immediately tighten it up so the dog is tugged towards them. This gives a dog an immediate excuse to resist and something to pull against.

Getting your dog to walk on a relaxed lead

Your aim is to get your dog to walk on a *relaxed* lead. So start out that way.

- Clip the lead onto your puppy and walk with him around your home or in your garden. Give him praise and rewards as he is walking along. Puppies like to follow their owners, so he should be keen to move in the direction that you are moving.
- As soon as he tugs on the lead or pulls, stop in your tracks. Be calm and wait for him to stop tugging.
- When he does, when the lead is relaxed and he is looking up at you, praise him and move off again.

Change direction

Another method you can try is to reverse direction.

- If he pulls, you simply turn and walk the other way. As you turn, lower your body slightly and motivate your dog to follow you by saying LET'S GO in a high tone of voice. Praise him when he follows you.
- Repeating this exercise will teach your puppy not to pull. It will also teach him that walking on a lead doesn't hurt, because as soon as he feels tightness on his throat, you stop or walk the other way. By not giving in to the pulling, you avoid reinforcing the behaviour.

- When you take your dog outside into the wide world, keep the training going. You can tighten the lead a little to motivate your dog to walk closer by your side when you cross a busy road. Always give him plenty of praise for walking well.
- Remember that every member of the family has to be consistent and use the same commands when they are walking the dog.

Leaving the house

Once dog walking is part of your daily routine, your dog will look forward to this part of the day with huge anticipation. As the hour approaches, he will notice every single sign that a walk is imminent and respond by displaying excited behaviour. Some dogs run about in circles, some yap, some run back and forth to the door. In the wild, pack members display similar behaviour before setting off on the hunt.

Of course your dog is going to be excited when he knows he's about to go out. But you shouldn't let this become an issue of control.

Preparing to go out:

- Your dog should sit before you put on the lead. Don't allow him to jump up. If he does, wait until you have his attention, ask him to sit again, and then put on the lead.
- Once the lead is on, many dogs immediately pull in the direction of the door. Don't allow your dog to do this. If he pulls, stop. Wait until he is paying attention to you before moving on.
- When you get to the door, ask your dog to sit. Then open the door a little. If your dog charges at it, shut it again. Repeat until you get to the point where you can open the door completely while the dog sits still.
- Walk out the door. If he pulls, stop and wait until the lead is relaxed again.

Heel!

Cue or signal: Slap your left thigh (or your right) depending on which side you feel most comfortable walking the dog.

Once your dog is walking well on a lead, you can teach him how to heel. Heeling is a refinement. When you're out walking your dog, you should not keep him walking to heel all of the time. But it is a very useful command when you are walking in crowded streets where there are many potential distractions or when your dog is off the lead in the park and you want to bring him back to you for whatever reason. Teach your dog to heel on the lead first, then teach him off the lead.

Here's how it works:

- Choose on which side you feel most comfortable walking your dog. For me, it's the left.
- Now imagine an invisible box attached to the left side of your leg.
- Walk with your dog normally. When your dog comes into that box, as soon as his shoulders are by your left thigh, give him praise and a reward.
- Then attach a sound and a signal to the action. As your dog comes into the box, slap your left thigh and say HEEL.
- When you change direction, slap your thigh and say HEEL just as you turn.

Here's a slightly different way of doing it:

- Put your dog on the lead.
- Then let your arm drop by your side, palm facing backwards.
- Your dog will naturally want to investigate. When he touches your palm with his nose, say GOOD BOY and treat. Repeat a few times.
- Vary the exercise a little. Hold your hand out for a few seconds and remove it.
- I sometimes use the command TOUCH. Or I might use no words at all.
- When your dog is touching your palm every time you put your hand down, add the command HEEL and pat your left (or right) leg.

If I am training very small dogs to heel, I sometimes use a target stick so I don't have to bend over so far. I wrap material around the bottom of the marker to bulk it out a little and make it easier for the dog to see. Instead of the dog touching my hand with his nose when he comes to heel, he touches the end of the target stick.

Other useful commands

Basic commands, such as COME, STAY and WATCH ME, are invaluable when you are exercising your dog, particularly when he is free running. It's never too early to start this kind of obedience training – and it's never too late to learn. LEAVE IT (see page 125) is also useful when you're out and about.

Come!

Cue or signal: Pat your chest or your legs. Or turn your body in the direction you want the dog to come.

The COME command is the most important of all. Start teaching your puppy to come when you call as soon as you bring him home. Use the same basic procedure as you would for teaching him to sit (see page 120), building up from a short distance of about 3 feet/1 metre away to greater distances. Teach him to come to you in the house before you try to teach him to come to you outdoors.

Make sure that you are touching your dog before you praise and reward him for coming to you. This tells him that he only gets a reward when he's that close, not a foot or so away.

A good way of teaching this command and making it fun is to play hide and seek. Dogs are good at this game and really enjoy it. Hide somewhere in the house and call him to come to you. Praise him when he finds you.

Puppies naturally like to stay pretty close to their owners. When you start training him to come to you outside, make use of that fact. Let him off the lead and practise the command in the garden or the park if it's safe to do so.

Sooner or later, however, your dog is going to demonstrate a little more independence.

Here's what to do:

- Teach him to come to you when you're outside by giving him a jackpot treat. Most dogs interpret your call to COME as the end of their fun. That's because they've worked out that when you call them to COME you usually put them on the lead and take them home. Change your dog's expectations. Call him to COME, give him a food treat, and let him go off and play again. Two treats for the price of one!
- Don't just stand there and call your dog to COME. Make yourself more attractive to him by walking or running in the direction you want him to go. Dogs are predisposed to chase and most will happily play this game. Don't sound harsh or serious when you give the command. Make your voice high and excited. I like to use the kind of chirping, clacking sounds that people use to urge horses to move faster.
- Exploit your dog's curiosity. If you don't feel like running, sit or lie down on the ground. Most dogs will come running to find out why you are lying there. Give your dog lots of treats to reassure him that nothing is the matter.
- Don't be unreasonable. Your dog is not going to come if he's playing with other dogs. Wait until there's a lull in the action before giving the command.
- Never, ever, ever tell a dog off if he is slow in responding to your command to come. Many owners get anxious or angry in this situation. The very last thing you should do is let him see or hear those

negative responses. If you tell him off when he does eventually come to you, you've just taught him not to come when he's called. You have to be a good actor. When he does come to you, however long it takes, praise him.

- Never, ever chase a dog when you want him to come to you. However, there may be occasions when you have no option but to run after him. In this case, drop treats behind you as you go, then make your way back to the first treat and hope that, if you have lost him, his nose will lead him back to you.

Watch me!

Cue or signal: Raise your hand to your eyes.
WATCH ME allows you to get your dog's attention when you're out and about, if there are children around, or if there are other kinds of distraction that might make him nervous. Here, you follow the same kind of procedure as you would for teaching him to SIT (see page 120), but you first place the treat in front of his nose and then take it up to your eye – this becomes the hand signal. Most dogs will look you in the eye if a tasty piece of chicken is dangling beside it. As when teaching SIT, repeat until he can also respond to the command without a treat.

Stay!

Cue or signal: Stretch your hand out in front of you, palm facing outwards.
The secret of teaching your dog to STAY is not to move through the stages too fast. Build it up gradually, both lengthening the time and distance. Unlike other commands, you can repeat the STAY command without undermining the training. That's because you're not asking your dog to take a specific action, and to take it promptly. Instead, you're asking the dog to do nothing at all.

Here's what to do:

- Put your dog into a sit position and stand in front of him.
- Put your palm near his face and say STAY. Wait a second and reward.
- Repeat and gradually lengthen the time between the command and reward until he is staying for ten seconds.
- Then you can take a step back. If your dog moves to follow you, give a correction – UH OH! – and try again.
- Slowly lengthen the distance between you. Always go back to the dog and don't praise or reward him until you are physically close to him again. Praising from a distance will encourage him to come to you, which undermines what you are trying to teach him.

Exercise problems

Many of the more common problems people have exercising their dogs stem from inadequate training. As I mentioned before, walking on a lead is not a natural behaviour for a dog, but it's a skill he needs to live in our world. Start training at an early age and take every opportunity to reinforce the lessons in different locations and under different conditions so he responds right on cue every time you want him to.

Pulling on the lead

Dogs that pull on the lead don't just give their owners arm-ache, they can also hurt their throats. If your dog is a persistent puller, chances are you haven't trained him properly. Once he's been doing this for a while, you may need some aids to break him out of the habit.

Two walking aids I would recommend for persistent pullers are the no-pull harness and the gentle leader. The no-pull harness has two padded straps that fit around the dog's front legs. The lead is attached just behind the dog's neck. When he pulls, he has the sensation of being lifted off the ground, which is usually enough to make him stop.

The gentle leader works like a halter on a horse. A nose loop fits around the muzzle. The lead is attached to a loop under the chin or to a loop at the side. When the dog pulls, his head automatically comes to the side and where the head goes, the body follows.

Using a gentle leader

- Never jerk the lead or you could hurt the dog's head.
- Make sure the noseband fits snugly but is not too tight. The dog should be able to pant and drink with it on.
- Never leave a gentle leader on an unsupervised dog.
- Get your dog used to the feel of the leader gradually. Put it on and take it off in the house, giving treats and praise. Then attach the lead and walk the dog around the house, rewarding calm behaviour.
- If your dog really struggles after a couple of days' practice or shows signs of anxiety such as excessive panting, urination or refusing to walk, you'll have to try a different method.

Refusing to walk

Refusing to walk, like refusing to eat, is not normal dog behaviour. Most dogs love their daily walks and a dog that won't budge an inch is trying to tell you something.

What's he trying to say? Rule out any physical causes first. He may be ill or in pain. He may be tired. The pavement may be too hot or too cold. He may be frightened of something. Puppies often plant their bottoms on the ground when they've been startled by a sudden noise, such as a fire engine tearing past. Don't yank your dog to his feet or offer him a treat. Rewarding your dog for showing signs of fear around a fire engine will only encourage him to repeat the behaviour next time.

I once worked with a boxer in New York who was absolutely terrified of garbage trucks. Every time the truck appeared in his street he would sit down on the pavement and refuse to move. Luckily, there are some very cooperative and understanding refuse workers in that city. The first week, I waited until the truck had turned down the next street, then I sat on the pavement with the dog while the dustmen came over, petted him and gave him treats. The second week we worked on getting a little closer to the truck – and all its lovely smells! I reinforced his calm behaviour with treats and praise. After that, each time the dustmen saw the dog, they would throw him treats until he came to associate the garbage truck with good things.

Running off

Losing a dog is every owner's worst nightmare. A dog that runs off and won't come back when he's called could be heading for danger or he might get himself well and truly lost. This is why having your dog micro-chipped is so important.

If your dog is in the habit of running away when he's off the lead you need to work harder teaching him the COME command. Many dogs will hare off into the distance, however, if they see something worth chasing. Persistent chasers may have to be exercised in safe fenced areas or on extendable leads.

When your dog runs off don't race after him unless you absolutely have to. That turns running off into a game of chase, which, let's face it, the dog's going to win. Instead make a loud distracting noise. When your dog turns around to find out what the fuss is about, lie on the ground. Most dogs will trot back to investigate. When he does, praise and reward him. Don't show him that you are angry or anxious.

If you have no option but to run after your dog, try to do so without letting him see you are chasing him. Drop treats on the ground as you go. If he disappears from sight, go back to the first treat and wait to see if his nose brings him back to you.

Aggression on the lead

Even mild-mannered, well-socialised dogs sometimes act aggressively on the lead, lunging out seemingly with no warning. What provokes this type of behaviour is usually fear – of another dog or a person who makes your dog feel uneasy. If your dog were off the lead he would probably run away. As he can't, he will try the next best thing, which is an aggressive display.

If your dog behaves like this a few times, you need to break the habit. Watch out for approaching dogs (or other sources of trouble) and cross the road or change direction to put some distance between you and them. Make a distracting noise, ask your dog to sit and watch you, then do some obedience exercises with him to keep his attention focused on you. When the other dog has passed and your dog has remained calm, give him a big treat.

Dogs behaving badly

I recently worked with a pair of Old English sheepdogs that were very badly behaved when together and on their leads. Bumble and Dougal were brother and sister. If they were walked together they barked constantly, scaring other dogs and people in the park. Individually on and off the lead they were fine. It was when they were together and on their leads that they were double trouble.

It seemed to me that some sort of pack behaviour was triggering the barking and excitable display. I decided that the best way to tackle it was to tire the dogs out so they simply wouldn't have the energy to misbehave. The owners were a mother and daughter, both teachers, and they lived by the sea. I asked the mother to exercise one dog on the beach for an hour. We put Bumble in a life jacket so she could paddle safely in the water. Meanwhile, the daughter was exercising Dougal by getting him to run alongside her while she cycled.

When we took the dogs back to the park after their workouts and let them off their leads, they were able to greet other dogs without ganging up on them. The extra exercise had dispelled all their negative emotions.

Special exercise regimes

A dog that is badly out of condition or overweight needs to be eased back to fitness in a controlled exercise programme. In such cases, you may also need the advice of a specialist such as a trained canine physiotherapist to determine how best to go about exercising your dog safely. A full medical check-up is also advisable beforehand.

Hydrotherapy

Swimming has been used for many years as a remedial therapy in veterinary practice and as a way of conditioning racehorses and racing greyhounds. Canine hydrotherapy for pet dogs is a relatively recent phenomenon.

Swimming is particularly good for obese dogs as it provides aerobic exercise without putting too much pressure on the dog's joints. It's also good for arthritic dogs or dogs who are getting older.

One of the dogs I've worked with was an extremely overweight dachshund called Jess, whose owner equated giving her love with giving her food, particularly all sorts of chews and treats that were high in fat and calories. The first thing that I did was to get rid of the 'Magic Cupboard' where all those goodies were kept. The second thing was to take Jess for some hydrotherapy.

Jess, supported by a life jacket and at either side by two trained physios, started on one lap of the pool three times a week. As she got fitter, that was increased to three laps. Finally the jacket could come off and she swam by herself, but there were always people in the pool with her.

If you want to try hydrotherapy for your pet, make sure the pool is a registered facility. Most pools prefer a direct referral from a vet. Registered pools should have good water quality and properly trained staff. Pools also vary in size and construction – some will be suitable for small dogs, others for large ones.

Treadmills

Gizmo, a male Chihuahua, lived in a family with lots of other dogs. Every day the other dogs would go off to run in the open fields at the back of the house, but Gizmo would get halfway down the garden and have to turn back because he just didn't have the puff to carry on. He was just like a kid who had been left behind at playtime.

Gizmo's favourite food was Indian takeaway and he was very obese as a consequence. When I put him on the scales to show his owner just how bad the problem was, he weighed the same as three Chihuahuas of a normal size.

It was time to get Gizmo fit again. I put him on a diet – strictly no naan bread or pappadums! – and I got him working out on a treadmill. Not the human kind, but a special canine treadmill of the sort that has been used to develop muscle tone and good coat condition in show dogs. I set Gizmo's treadmill up alongside the owner's and they worked out together.

Canine treadmills are available in different sizes to suit different breeds; you can also hire them. We started with very short sessions and gradually increased the workouts until Gizmo was fit again and could keep up with the other dogs.

Keep fit with your dog

Why not share your favourite exercise with your dog? If you jog, your dog can jog with you. If you cycle, he can run alongside.

Exercise some common sense as well as your muscles. Dogs with very short legs or whose pace is very different to yours won't be comfortable jogging and might not be able to keep up with the bike. Build sessions up slowly and monitor your dog's responses. Always take plenty of water with you and give your dog small, frequent drinks.

If you are cycling with your dog, stay away from roads and exercise in safe areas in the park. It's better to cycle with your dog running free to prevent the lead getting tangled up in the wheels.

chapter six
good game!

This chapter is all about the many different ways you can have fun with your dog. What, you may ask, does fun have to do with your dog's health and fitness? More than you might think.

Feeding your dog the right diet and making sure he gets enough exercise will help maintain him in peak physical condition throughout his life. But fun and games are also important for your dog's wellbeing in the fullest sense of the word. Mental stimulation keeps a dog alert, banishes boredom and gives him the chance to do what he likes best – which is interact with you.

Dogs are social animals with a very real need for affection and company. A dog that was fed and exercised properly but shut alone in a room the rest of the time would be very unhappy. His physical needs would be met, but little else in his life would give him pleasure or stimulation. Dogs that are deprived in this way quickly resort to all kinds of activities that we humans label 'problem behaviours'. They may become destructive, chewing or ripping up everything in sight. They may develop compulsions, such as excessive licking or tail chasing. Or they may vocalise their misery by hours of barking or howling. They resort to such activities because there is nothing else for them to do and it's a way of soothing themselves and relieving their frustration.

Dogs need to play, or perhaps I should say they need to work. A dog doesn't distinguish between the two. Only human beings arrange their lives into such hard and fast categories. Whether a dog is trying to get food out of a rubber toy, or rolling over on command, or fetching that Frisbee you threw across the park, he's working hard, using his mental skills as well as his physical ones. He's also having the time of his life.

We could learn a lot from dogs. Teach your dog new skills, enjoy the time you spend together and it won't just be your dog that will benefit.

Positive training

A dog doesn't distinguish between giving his paw and sitting or staying when he's asked to. He's simply using his mental skills to perform certain tasks and enjoying the opportunity to interact with you.

Find your dog's motivator

What gets your dog going? For many dogs, it's food, which is why food treats are usually so effective as rewards in training or for good behaviour. Food isn't the only canine motivator, however. Dogs will work hard for what gives them pleasure, including toys and games. A good reward for a dog is often the chance to keep on playing. Just think how many dogs will ask their owners to play fetch with them by bringing over a ball or stick and dropping it invitingly at their feet.

In previous chapters, I've given instructions on how to teach commands such as SIT, COME, LEAVE IT, and so on. Here are some other ones you could try.

Down!

Cue or signal: Start by placing the flat of your hand on the ground. Later on, you can just lower your hand.

After you have taught a dog to sit, you can teach him to lie down. Very big dogs, such as Great Danes, find lying down and getting up again very strenuous and I wouldn't recommend making them do it too often.

- Use a treat and put your dog into a sit.
- Place your hand, with the treat in it, palm down on the floor and let your dog sniff it but don't let him have it. At this stage, don't give a command or say anything at all.
- Your dog will be working out how to get the treat from your hand. As soon as he lies down on his belly, give him the treat and praise him.
- Repeat the same procedure two more times. Wait for the action, catch it, give him the treat and praise him.
- The next step is to put in the vocal cue and signal. As your dog is in the act of lying down, say DOWN and lower your hand, palm down, onto the floor. Repeat this five to ten times.
- Finally say DOWN using the hand signal before he has even started to lie down.
- If he gets it wrong, say UH OH! and repeat the exercise. Release your dog by saying OK when you want him to get up again.

Shake!

Cue or signal: A cupped hand.
This is the way I teach a dog how to give his paw.

Here's what to do:

- Put your dog into a sit and place a treat on his nose.
- Your dog will naturally raise his paw to try to knock the treat from his nose. When he does so, say GOOD BOY and let him have the treat.
- After you have repeated these stages five times, begin to put the command SHAKE with the action. Say it just as your dog is in the act of lifting his paw and accompany the command with the signal of a cupped hand.
- Repeat these stages five more times.
- Now you can forget about the treat on the nose and carry on practising the command. If your dog does not lift his paw when you ask him to, say UH OH! and remove the treat from view.
- When the dog is lifting his paw more often than not, you can slip your hand down underneath it once it is raised. Don't hold onto the paw, just support it lightly.
- Always end the training session on a positive note when he has been successful.

Roll over!

Cue or signal: A circling finger.
This is a trick you can teach a dog once he has mastered the DOWN command.

Here's what to do:

- Put your dog into a sit and then give him the DOWN command.
- Crouch down beside your dog, right by his head, and place a treat beside his nose.
- Circle the treat over his nose.
- The dog will naturally roll over as he tries to follow the treat.
- When he rolls over, say GOOD BOY and give him the treat.
- After you have repeated these stages five times, begin to put the command ROLL OVER with the action. Say it just as your dog is in the act of rolling over and accompany the command with the signal of a circling finger.
- Repeat these stages five more times.
- Now you can start to ask him to ROLL OVER without circling the treat around his nose. Praise and reward him when he gets it right. When he doesn't, say UH OH! and remove the treat from view.
- End each session on a positive note.

Fetch!

No hand signal.

You're going with the flow if you teach your retriever to fetch, because that's what these dogs are bred to do. But even retrievers won't retrieve if what you are throwing for them is not worth fetching.

I was once told about a retriever who wouldn't retrieve. The dog came from a long line of accomplished bird retrievers, but was showing absolutely no sign of following in the family tradition. His owners tried everything – dumbbells, treat balls, toys – but nothing would persuade that retriever to retrieve. Finally, in sheer desperation, the owners decided to try the exercise with a real dead bird. Bingo! The dog brought it straight back the first time.

There are many ways to teach a dog to fetch, but this is one of my favourites.

Here's what to do:

- Start by showing your dog a toy or some other object that he likes but that is not too valuable to him to be given up.
- As soon as your dog puts his mouth over the toy, ask him to TAKE IT.
- Play with your dog for a while.
- After a couple of minutes, ask the dog to drop the toy into your hand, using the DROP IT command.
- When he releases the toy, praise him.
- Then throw the toy on the ground a small distance away. As soon as he puts his mouth on it, say TAKE IT, and praise him again.
- Then it's playtime again.
- After a few minutes, ask your dog to drop the toy, using the DROP IT command. He should drop the toy into your hand. When he does, praise him and reward him.
- Repeat the sequence, throwing the toy greater distances each time you play the game.
- When your dog is good at playing the game, use toys or objects of higher value and that are therefore more stimulating to retrieve.

Anyone for tennis?

Anything that makes a ball go further gives your dog a better workout when he's playing fetch. I often take a tennis racket along to the park with me – I can hit a ball a lot further than I can throw it. Frisbees are also good for games of fetch. Another useful aid is a ball-catcher, which is basically a long stick with a cup on the end of it. You use the stick to hurl the ball a long way and the cup comes in handy for picking it up when the dog brings it back.

Brainwaves

The reason why mental stimulation is a good way of relieving emotional or behavioural problems in a dog has to do with the way the brain is structured. There are two main systems in a dog's brain – the limbic system, which governs the emotions, and the cerebral cortex, which is involved in problem-solving. These two systems enjoy an inverse relationship to each other. When a dog is in the grip of a powerful emotion, the limbic system is in overdrive and the cerebral cortex is shut down. That means the dog literally can't learn. The opposite is also true. When you stimulate a dog mentally, the limbic system is deactivated and he is distracted from negative emotions that would otherwise overwhelm him, stop him from learning and lead to problem behaviours.

When I'm working with a dog that suffers from emotional problems such as aggression, anxieties or obsessions, I use obedience training as a means of distracting the dog at a time his emotions would normally be triggered. For example, if a dog has got into the habit of barking at strangers, I will work with the dog on a sequence of commands as someone is coming through the door.

The key is anticipation. You have to engage the dog before the stimulus takes hold and he falls back on his usual response. Given time, this type of training will correct the behaviour. Instead of the dog barking as soon as he hears a stranger at the door, for example, he will look forward to making a connection with his owner and gaining a treat.

Go find!

No hand signal.

Games of hide and seek are great for dogs. When your puppy is small you can help to teach him to COME by hiding yourself in the house and calling him to come and find you. Hiding food around the house at dinner-time is another good way of stimulating a dog to use his brain. It isn't cruel – it's simply encouraging natural behaviour. In the wild, all dogs have to work for their food.

You can also play games of hide and seek with toys, either indoors or out in the garden. Hounds and other dogs that hunt by scent are good at this game. To teach this game, you'll need the help of another person to hold the dog and a number of toys of increasing value – to the dog, that is.

Here's what to do:

- Start by making it easy. While your friend or partner is holding the dog, show the dog the lowest value toy. Let him sniff it. Then let him see you hide it somewhere close by. Make it clear how exciting this game is going to be.
- Release the dog and encourage him to go and get the toy. GO FIND! You can go along with him, praising him as he gets closer.
- When the dog finds the toy, the reward is getting it and carrying on with the game. Praise him.
- Make it clear that the fun game will only carry on if the first toy is brought back. Show him another toy of slightly higher value to encourage him to come back to you.
- Repeat the game, hiding the second toy a little further away.

Social skills

Playing with your dog is a good way to teach him the social skills he needs to live in your world. With puppies you have a relatively small window of opportunity to introduce him to his new environment. Up to the age of about 16 weeks, puppies are naturally curious and eager to explore. After 16 weeks, which is the age when they would have started to fend for themselves, they become more wary. It's a basic survival mechanism.

As soon as you get your puppy home, introduce him to as many new things as possible. Don't overwhelm him with different sensations, but make sure he has the broadest exposure to his new surroundings that you can give him. Use food and treats to reinforce the idea that these new experiences mean pleasure.

Get your puppy used to your touch, to other people, including children, and to other dogs. Take him to other locations outside the home – the vet's, the surrounding streets, a number of parks and other open spaces. Take him on car journeys – or on the bus, if that's going to be the way you get around.

Get your puppy used to your touch, to other people, including children, and to other dogs.

Biting in puppies

When you're playing with your dog you can teach him bite-inhibition at the same time. Puppies explore their world through 'mouthing' like human babies do. But they need to learn that it is unacceptable to chew on you. A playful puppy bite can have much more serious consequences when the adult teeth come in. Let your puppy chew on his toys, but as soon as he chews on you, give a short, sharp yelp – OUCH! – to warn him off. If he carries on, ignore him and leave the room for a moment. Carry on until he understands that biting stops play.

Doggy playmates

Dogs make great company for each other. You don't have to rush out and get another dog, you can simply team up with another dog-owner in your neighbourhood or who frequents the same park. Dogs gain tremendous exercise by playing with each other. From the first introduction – the play bow – when a dog will signal his friendliness and willingness to play by dropping down on his front legs – to the time when you clip the lead back on and take him home, happy and tired, he'll have a great time romping with a canine friend. The best match for your dog will be another that shares his energy levels, build and general disposition.

I once worked with a boxer called Zulu that found it hard to get on with other dogs. He had been brought to Britain from South Africa at the age of two. In South Africa dogs are generally kept in backyards and this had been the case with Zulu. As a result he had no idea how to behave around other dogs. Zulu was quite a dominant individual. At first I thought another dominant dog would be a good match for him, but when I introduced him to a forceful female boxer, it was clear that was not going to work. The two just snapped at each other and I had to separate them. Then I brought in a more submissive female boxer to see what would happen.

It was fascinating. At first Zulu tried his old trick and snapped at her. In response, she laid back on her belly in a submissive, pacifying gesture. After sniffing her for ten minutes, Zulu was in love. He started to follow her everywhere. In the end he was licking her ears and muzzle and lying beside her. What the submissive boxer had done was to teach Zulu the pacification signals other dogs use to show they are no threat. His aggressive behaviour had stemmed from a lack of confidence on his part – he just didn't know how to communicate with other dogs.

Keeping dogs busy

Dogs should never be left alone for long periods. To deprive a social animal of company is just plain cruelty. Few reputable breeders will even sell a pup to a prospective owner unless they have satisfied themselves that someone will be home most of the time to be with the dog. Four to six hours is the most you should leave your dog alone.

Of course, all dog owners have to leave their dogs for some periods during the day. There are various ways you can prevent your dog from becoming anxious and bored in your absence.

Points to consider:

- Make sure your dog is exercised and has had a chance to poo and pee before you leave.
- Fill a feeder cube or treat ball with the dried portion of the dog's regular food. Dogs can spend many happy hours trying to figure out how to get those tasty morsels out of the toys. Remember to cut back on the next meal accordingly.
- Don't make a big deal out of leaving or returning. Withdraw your attention from your dog gradually 20 minutes before you leave the house and ignore any excessive displays of greeting when you return.
- Keep lights on and the radio or TV playing so the dog does not experience a total change in his environment.

Older dogs

When your dog gets on in years he may find it hard to exercise at the same levels he was used to. That's no excuse for him to be bored. Play remains important throughout life and old age is no exception. Training and games inside the home can make up for what an older dog is missing in the way of stimulation outside. You can also drive your dog to the park instead of walking him there and just let him explore new smells and sensations at his own pace. I've even taken old dogs out for drives in the car just to give them something new to look at.

Outward bound

Your dog's breed makeup can direct you to suitable activities, fun and games that he will enjoy. Retrievers, spaniels and other dogs bred as sporting companions are naturally going to like playing hide and seek, which is very similar to the type of work they would do in the field. Dalmatians do very well in endurance trials, which is not surprising since they were originally bred to cover long distances running along roads beside carriages, which is why they are known as 'carriage dogs'.

Blowing bubbles and other fun games

Activities that combine a good workout with mental stimulation really make for happy, contented dogs. In one of my programmes I hired a special doggy bubble machine that blew bacon-flavoured bubbles. Red and Rusty, the two retrievers I was working with, had the time of their lives chasing the bubbles all over the garden. (If you want to do the same, make sure the liquid used to make the bubbles is safe for dogs.)

In another family, I taught the kids how to play a simple game with their Dalmatian, Dally. Dally, who also features in an earlier chapter, was highly intelligent but food-obsessed and needed to have her focus redirected through play and stimulation. The kids stood at either end of the garden throwing a tennis ball to each other while Dally dashed between them trying to catch it. Every so often one of the kids would throw the ball up into the air so Dally could catch it. That was her reward – and she'd earned it. To show the game was carrying on, I told the kids to make an effort to touch her every time she went past or caught the ball. But no attempt was made to take the ball away from her. Instead, another ball was produced and the game carried on.

Tug of war is another impromptu game that many dogs enjoy, particularly breeds such as terriers. Before you play this game, I suggest that you make sure that the dog has been taught the DROP IT command. I would also stop the game immediately if the dog is showing signs of getting over-stimulated. Many people say that it is important that the owner should win a game of tug of war every time, otherwise the dog will think he is the dominant partner. In my experience, however, if you let go of the tug rope, the dog always comes back wanting more, which does not seem to indicate dominance to me. Make sure you play tug with a proper canine tug toy that won't fray easily.

Special activities

Special dog activities and events provide you with the opportunity to step up the training and really see what your dog is capable of. They're fun for owners as well as dogs. Do a little research or check with your particular breed organisation to find out which type of activity would benefit your dog and suit his energy levels and build.

What's on offer includes:

- Mock gun-dog trials for pointers, retrievers and spaniels.
- Scent-tracking for hounds.
- Carriage dog trials for Dalmatians. The ultimate test is an endurance run of 25 miles/40 km. There are also rules to observe regarding the proper way to run beside the horse and carriage.
- Agility classes, which consist of assault courses to negotiate. These are good for small active dogs such as Jack Russell terriers.
- Fly ball for active working dogs such as Border collies. The dog has to tackle a number of jumps before reaching a platform, where he has to learn how to depress a pedal to release a ball before bringing it back to his owner.
- 'Heel to music' is an American craze that is just reaching Britain. In this form of very advanced obedience training, owners use a combination of hand signals and vocal commands to teach dogs how to dance along with them to music in a set choreography. One of the dogs I've worked with, a Labrador/whippet mix with chronic separation anxiety, really benefited from this activity. It took away her anxiety and distress because her mind was on other things and it enabled her to bond with and focus on her owner in a better way.

Dance with your dog, teach him new tricks, but whatever you do – PLAY with him!

Contacts

Animal Health Trust
The science behind animal welfare. Information on pet care. Leaflets and publications.
www.aht.org.uk
t: 08700 50 24 24

Association of Pet Behaviour Counsellors
Network of qualified counsellors treating problem behaviour in pet animals.
www.apbc.org.uk

British Veterinary Association
National representative body for the British veterinary profession.
www.bva.co.uk
t: 020 7636 6541

Burns Dog Food
A range of dog food made without chemical colours and preservatives, cereal and animal derivatives.
www.burns-pet-nutrition.co.uk

Canine Concepts
Innovative dog supplies for dog training and sheer indulgence.
www.canineconcepts.co.uk

Canine and Feline Behaviour Association
Network of qualified practitioners treating problem behaviour.
www.cfba.co.uk

Canine Hydrotherapy Association
Hydrotherapy health treatment organisation. Provides listings of hydrotherapy pools throughout the UK.
www.k9hydrotherapy.co.uk
t: 07050 265971 – general enquiries

Celia Cross Greyhound Trust
Rescue and rehoming centre for greyhounds.
T: 01483 222832

Company of Animals
Specialists in behaviour and training products and advice.
www.companyofanimals.co.uk
t: 01932 566696 – for sales-related enquiries
t: 01932 574271/01932 574281 – for behaviour-related enquiries

Diana Brimblecombe Animal Rescue Centre
A registered charity based in Berkshire with a spacious and well-equipped rescue centre for dogs and other animals.
www.dbarc.org.uk
t: 0118 9341122

Fetch Pet
Dog toys and accessories.
www.fetchpet.co.uk
t: 01243 512123

James Wellbeloved
Produces a range of natural, hypoallergenic foods.
www.wellbeloved.co.uk

Lila Paws
Luxury accessories for dogs.
www.lilapaws.co.uk
t: 020 8541 5877

Lucies Farm
Luxury dog kennels and makers of gourmet natural dog food.
www.dog-hotel.co.uk

Marc Abraham
Brighton-based vet who is passionate about promoting responsible pet-ownership in the community, and actively supports a number of animal and wildlife charities.
www.marcthevet.com

Nature Diet
A range of high-quality natural food.
www.naturediet.net
t: 08700 132960

Pet Health Care
Comprehensive on-line source of pet care information. Guide to breeds. Pet insurance. On-line veterinary advice.
www.pethealthcare.co.uk

Pet Organic
Range of organic and natural pet foods and products for dogs, cats, small animals, horses and birds.
www.petorganic.com

Pet Planet
Wide range of products and on-line shopping for dogs, cats and small animals.
www.petplanet.co.uk

RSPCA
Royal Society for the Prevention of Cruelty to Animals. Publications, advice on animal care, rehoming, campaigns.
www.rspca.org.uk
t: 0870 55 55 999 – for 24-hour national cruelty and advice line
t: 0870 33 35 999 – to register for enquiries service

Southfields Hydrotherapy and Dog Grooming
Hydrotherapy healing and care centre for dogs in West London.
www.southfields.uk.com
t: 020 8995 2060

The Kennel Club
Information on training, special activities such as agility classes, guide to breeds and breed standards, dog clubs, finding breeders and choosing puppies.
www.the-kennel-club.org.uk
t: 0870 606 6750

Victoria Stilwell
Official website
www.victoriastilwell.com

The Wag and Bone Show
Annual dog show that hosts a vast array of fun activities, shows, training sessions and advice.
www.wagandboneshow.co.uk

Waterside Action Group
Group dedicated to ending the cruel practice of puppy farming. Also offers guidelines to prevent malpractice in the sale of dogs and puppies.
www.wag-ayrshire.org.uk

Index

Acknowledgements

First of all I would like to thank Van, Alex and all my family and friends for their love and continuing support. Thanks also to Denise Bates, to Liz Wilhide and all those at HarperCollins who have been so wonderful to me. To Mark Read for outstanding photography and Smith and Gilmour for beautiful design. To all the team at Ricochet and Channel 4 – you are an amazing group of people and it has been a real honour to work with you on It's Me or the Dog. Thanks to Marc 'the vet' Abraham who has helped me with this book and shares my passion to spread the word. To my agents Geraldine Woods and Jon Roseman. Thanks to all the families and dogs we have met during the filming of the show – you have helped get the knowledge out there and for that I am eternally grateful. And finally to all dogs fat and thin, I hope we do you justice.

The publishers would like to thank the following for kindly allowing us to feature their dogs in photography: Charlie, Jack and Millie Busby and Izzy, Jinnie Chalton Ena and Tosca, Melanie and Jeff Collier and Neo and Cookie, Louise Dyer and Alfie, James Hill and Bonnie and Harvey, Darren Middleditch and Maddie and Mungo, Anne O'Brien and Luka, Sheelagh O'Neill and Rosie, Amanda Pagliacci Lynch and Winnie, Michael Ruggins and Max, Georgie Smith and Jess, Gail Squibb and Freddie and Rhine, Lucy and Gerry Winfield and Snoop and Charlie.

Thank you also to the Diana Brimblecombe Animal Rescue Centre for Puppies, to Pet Planet (www.petplanet.co.uk) for supplying props for photography, to Southfields Hydrotherapy and Dog Grooming, and to Stag Lodge Stables, Richmond Park.